Dining with diplomats, praying with gunmen

Dining with diplomats, praying with gunmen

Experiences of international conciliation for a new generation of peacemakers

Anne Bennett

First published March 2020

Quaker Books, Friends House, 173 Euston Road, London NW1 2BJ

www.quaker.org.uk

Enquiries should be addressed to the Publications Manager,
Quaker Books, Friends House, 173 Euston Road, London NW1 2BJ.

© Anne Bennett 2020

ISBN: 978 1 99931 415 6

eISBN: 978 1 99931 416 3

Illustration and typesetting by Lynn Finnegan

Printed by RAP Spiderweb, Oldham

Printed on 100% recycled paper.

Contents

Foreword

Since the 17th century, Quakers have tried to live their faith according to principles or 'testimonies'. The core Quaker testimonies are peace, equality, simplicity, and integrity. These are interdependent prerequisites for building a more harmonious, compassionate and empathetic world. Peace without justice or equality is a precarious peace. Equality without simplicity and integrity is vulnerable and difficult to sustain in a capitalist world of high mass consumption. Integrity without peace, equality and simplicity is hypocrisy. Quaker principles, therefore, are challenged in the 21st century by a deeply divided, unequal, heavily militarised, and violent world.

At the heart of this excellent book is a very specific peace process that Quakers have utilised in their efforts to unite divided and violent societies and to prevent or stop wars between nations: conciliation. In particular, it is concerned with spiritually based conciliation aimed at ending suffering. Quaker experiences of national and international conciliation have sought to understand the origins of violence and the dynamics that might heal broken relationships. This conciliation process is seen as a contribution to an acknowledgement of differences, conflict prevention, co-existence, recognition of commonalities, and long-term reconciliation.

Quaker international conciliation has a long and distinguished history, perhaps beginning with initiatives to solve disputes in the 17th century between colonists and Native Americans on Rhode Island. Through civil society shuttle diplomacy in the Nigerian Civil War and long-term peacemaking in Sri Lanka, or bridging the divides in Northern Ireland, Quakers have been quietly enhancing their conciliatory peacemaking skills.

But what makes Quaker efforts distinctive from a host of other organisations dedicated to building peace by peaceful means?

In the first place, Quaker reverence for life and a commitment to absolute pacifism is something that parties in conflict appreciate and acknowledge.

Secondly, Quaker conciliators take great pains to generate 'safe spaces' for awkward and difficult conversations. Other groups do too, but there is something distinctive, reassuring and non-threatening about the ways Quakers create safe sanctuaries for dialogue, listening and attention. When my wife and I were co-directing the Quaker United Nations Office in Geneva we were always impressed by diplomats, representatives of armed actors and Non-Governmental Organisations asking for meetings at Quaker House because of its reputation for principled multipartiality.

Thirdly, unlike many other organisations that have funding for short periods of time, Quakers have built up a reputation for long-term commitments to parties and places in conflict. Peacemaking is a marathon, not a sprint, and those living under the shadow of violence want to know that outsiders have a long-term commitment.

Fourthly, because Quaker conciliators commit for the long haul, they are able to build trust and create ripe conditions for external accompaniment of local actors seeking to prevent, manage or end violent conflict.

Fifth, effective Quaker conciliators also understand the importance of going with the grain of locality and working with local people so that they are setting their own peacemaking agenda and getting credit and recognition for solving their own problems. As Sydney Bailey often said, Quaker intervenors should work to ensure that the parties to conflict get all the recognition for the success of an intervention and be willing to accept responsibility for their failures.

Sixth, because Quaker conciliation is spiritually based, its efforts are optimistic, loving and hopeful. These are all critical components for developing deep-rooted mutuality across boundaries of cultural and political difference.

Most of all, building peace is a never-ending process. Those of us who have made a professional commitment to peacemaking know that there are no perfect people, no perfect intervenors and no perfect interventions. We have to make do with good-enough solutions.

This book demonstrates that over the years Quakers have done more than that. Anne Bennett explores the full spread of Quaker experience, from dining with diplomats to praying with gunmen. The wisdom and experience of past Quaker peacemakers, the experiences of current practitioners and ideas from young peace-makers all come together in this excellent read. Together with the related consultation event, this book aims to help find a way forward and to capture the learning from quiet work that is carried out from a base of faith and is by its nature imperfect and often unfinished.

I commend this book to all who wish to understand how Friends have sought to build peace nationally and globally over many years.

Kevin Clements
Former Co-Director of QUNO Geneva
Foundation Director and Chair of the National Centre for
Peace and Conflict Studies, University of Otago, New Zealand

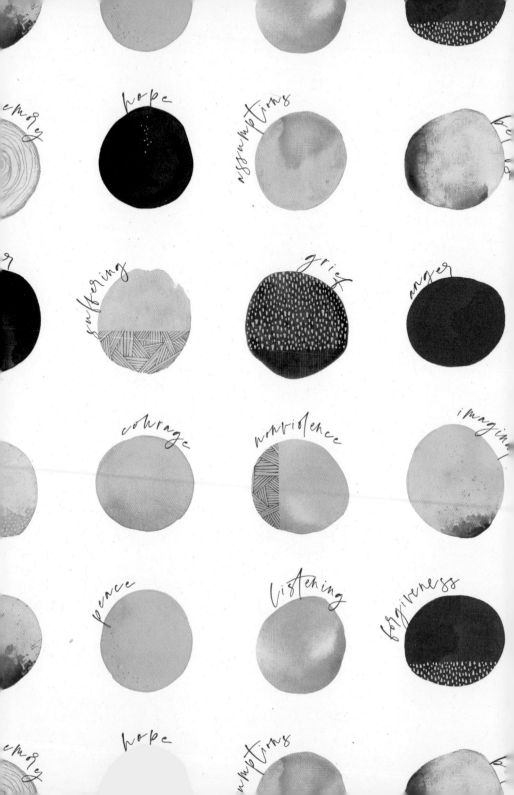

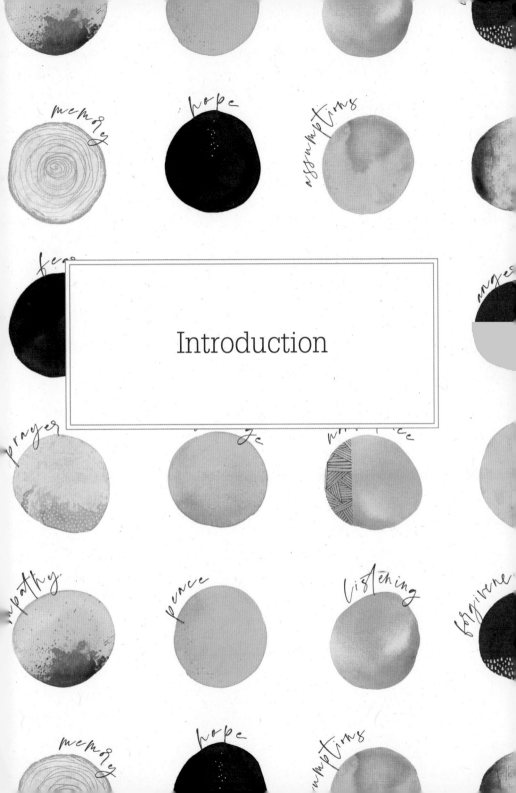

Introduction

During the Nigerian Civil War of 1967–1970, Quakers provided relief and rehabilitation programmes to both sides of the conflict. At one stage over 100 staff (mostly highly trained Nigerian people) were involved in what was the largest Quaker relief and rehabilitation programme since World War II. This practical, humanitarian work aimed to relieve suffering without furthering the aims of those involved with the civil war. Alongside this work, Quakers became convinced that the resolution of the conflict had to come through a negotiated settlement, and they worked to achieve this by assisting with the peace process.

A team of three Quakers – Adam Curle, Walter Martin and John Volkmar – were engaged in the conciliation process during a 30-month period. They paid repeated visits to government officials and leaders of the cessation group at the highest level while maintaining links with other international government organisations and the United Nations, all of which were trying to bring an end to the violent conflict. Their friendly and low-level approach, understanding of the cultural and ethnic issues, and willingness to take risks impressed those with whom they were working.

Conciliation has been defined by those involved in preparing for the Woodbrooke consultation as:

> The process of bringing people together and creating enough trust between them for them to talk constructively together. It usually involves the help of facilitators to encourage the parties to move to that point and to engage in dialogue to resolve the conflict that has divided them.

It is a slow-moving process that goes at the pace of the main participants and requires the long-term commitment of all involved.

Within Britain Yearly Meeting, there is ongoing national and local conciliation work with which Quakers are involved as individuals, in their meetings and through other Quaker Peace & Social Witness (QPSW) and Quaker Life programmes. There is also interchurch and interfaith work undertaken locally and at a national level. These Quakers use similar processes, which have been tested over the years. This book focuses on international Quaker conciliation and hopes to provide the reader with a greater understanding of the processes that form part of Quaker shared heritage, as well as what has happened in the past and where it might be used again in the future.

Quakers have a long history of involvement in international conciliation processes, building on their local and international networks. Much of this work is so confidential that its details never reach the public domain. In 1989, a consultation was organised by Quaker Peace & Service[1] at Jordans Quaker Centre in Buckinghamshire, where 21 experienced Quakers (including two facilitators) came together to look at where they had worked, their roles, and how the knowledge and skills they had developed could be transferred to a younger generation. This conference produced a confidential report outlining the discussions for use by those who had participated in the event but not for general circulation.

Thirty years later, the QPSW Conciliation Group took the bold step of organising another consultation, which took place in September 2019 at Woodbrooke Quaker Study Centre in Birmingham. The purpose of the Woodbrooke consultation was twofold: to provide an opportunity for an intergenerational exchange between Quaker peacemakers about international conciliation work past, present and future, and to capture the learning and ideas in a book.

---

1   The predecessor of Quaker Peace & Social Witness, a department of Britain Yearly Meeting.

The 42 participants consisted of two groups: older Quakers with considerable experience of international conciliation and younger Quakers involved in peacebuilding and with an interest in international conciliation but little or no practical experience. It was hoped that the consultation would generate energy and a sense of the way forward.

The vision of those organising the Woodbrooke consultation was that there should be an opening up of this valuable work among Friends. Rather than producing a report with limited circulation, there should be a book. The book would be a record of the consultation itself, drawing on the learning and insights of participants but also sharing this fascinating but little-known area of Quaker work. In producing such a book, care had to be taken to ensure that the confidential nature of the work was preserved, and every effort has been made to protect the identities of everyone involved.

The Quakers who worked with both sides in the Nigerian Civil War were engaged in a process that stretched over two and a half years, during which they built on existing Quaker networks and developed new connections:

> [The Quakers] were drawn into a conciliatory role which they sustained with sensitivity, flexibility and imagination, and without making mistakes serious enough to detract from the whole effort. ... The peace terms ... were imbued with the spirit of conciliation.
>
> (Yarrow, 1978: p. 259)

As Mike Yarrow says elsewhere in his book, the credit for the peace terms belongs to the Nigerians. But perhaps there was an element of truth in the observations of those who also saw traces of Quaker influence on the process.

Details of this type of work are dealt with in this book, highlighting the slow, determined process and the challenges faced by the teams. It is hoped that this book will convey to the reader a sense of why, where, how and when such work takes place, and also increase the reader's knowledge of the processes, Quaker heritage and options for the future.

Conciliation is the process of bringing people together and creating enough trust between them for them to talk constructively together.

Chapter 1

A brief history of Quaker international conciliation

An early example of Quakers interceding in a conflict in which they had no direct links with either side occurred in 1850, when two Quakers and a peace leader – Joseph Sturge, Frederick Wheeler and Elihu Burritt respectively – responded to a request for help to resolve the Schleswig-Holstein dispute. The key issue in the dispute was whether the Duchy of Schleswig was part of Denmark or whether, along with Holstein, it should become part of the German Confederation. It was a significant conflict with a long and complicated history. However, while attending a peace congress in Frankfurt, the three men saw an opportunity for them to make a contribution by setting up a quiet process to engage with both sides in the violent conflict. Mike Yarrow describes the process:

> The team prepared for their task by listening to a number of people in Hamburg and Berlin who could tell them about the issues and give them introductions to top officials on the Schleswig side. In the midst of the activities they found time to 'sit down in silence together'. With appropriate Quaker understatement, Joseph Sturge wrote, 'I feel little expectation of any benefit arising from the attempt, except the conviction that we have done what we can to prevent the continuance of war. I hope that we shall do no harm.'

> With strong support from Germans who had identified themselves with the cause of the Duchies, they found no difficulty in travelling through the military checkpoints to the embattled town of Rendsburg, where the officials greeted them cordially. The leaders of the provisional government did not want to make a public move toward negotiation, fearing that it would be taken as a sign of weakness by the enemy and by their people in the heat of a war they thought they could win, but they indicated confidentially their willingness

to refer their claims to impartial arbitration provided that suitable signs came from Denmark.

Travelling then by boat to Copenhagen, the peacemakers secured an interview with the Danish prime minister. A major obstacle in the minds of the Danes was that they did not want to concede to the Schleswig-Holsteiner rebels the semblance of international status implied by seeking an outside arbitrator.

After further talks a distinguished citizen from each side was appointed to confer on the constitution and terms of reference of a court of arbitration. At this point the Quaker team went home feeling that it had achieved its aims.

(Yarrow, 1978: pp. 17–19)

Sadly, the proposal had no opportunity to progress: within weeks, Austria and Prussia, with the support of Britain, France and Russia, settled the conflict by maintaining the status quo and forcing both Schleswig and Holstein to remain with Denmark. Mike Yarrow writes:

The Quaker effort had been based on the hope that a just peace could be brought about by arbitration between the two parties at war, but the issue had been greatly complicated by the rivalries among the ruling groups of France, Russia, Britain, Austria, and Prussia, which were attempting to maintain stability in Europe by channelling or curbing, in their own interest, the emerging forces of liberalism and nationalism. The lesson for future conciliators was to study carefully the international entanglement as well as the merits of the case.

(Yarrow, 1978: p. 19)

It arose from their deeply held commitment to peace, which to them was not just an idea or a philosophy but a belief of 'that of God in everyone' that should lead to action.

The involvement of Sturge, Wheeler and Burritt in the process may on one level have appeared both courageous and naïve. However, it arose from their deeply held commitment to peace, which to them was not just an idea or a philosophy but a belief of 'that of God in everyone' that should lead to action. Respect for Quakers and their peace testimony had opened doors and provided the opportunity for this small team to engage with a violent conflict.

Earlier still in history, this commitment to peace led to the first known recorded involvement of Quakers in a conciliation process, which was an attempt by Rhode Island Quakers to stop a war between colonists and Native Americans in 1675. Many other examples of involvement in conciliation followed, including the visit of a small team of Quakers to the Tsar of Russia in 1854 to try to find ways to prevent the outbreak of war in the Crimea.

All of these efforts towards international conciliation were built on several core principles: they were undertaken by a small team that was prepared to travel, engage in the process by building trust, listen to the demands of both sides and work with everyone to find a sustainable solution. A body of skills and knowledge was developed, and this has continued to be used and refined along with other tools that have supported the process. These have evolved over the years and will be explored in more detail in later chapters of this book.

After World War I, a number of Quaker centres were established in Europe, including in Nuremberg, Paris, Vienna, and Warsaw. Initially founded to provide relief, they turned their attention to peacemaking as this need diminished. Each centre responded to the needs of the country in which it was situated, with the aim of trying to prevent future wars. During the 1930s, for example, the Quaker centres in Berlin and Warsaw organised conferences and meetings to ease the tensions between the Germans and the Poles. Later, with the rise of the Nazi Party in Germany, attention was moved to the plight of the Jews and a number of schemes were developed to help them leave the country. Then, in 1922, a Quaker centre was opened in Switzerland to support the newly founded League of Nations.

All of these centres provided Quakers with opportunities to acquire detailed knowledge of international situations and to develop relationships with those engaged with issues at national and international levels. As a result, the Quakers became better placed to determine areas where they might usefully play a role. This information was shared among those Quakers personally involved but also among a wider Quaker audience through articles and talks. In this way, awareness grew and the body of people with the skills to undertake such work expanded.

After World War II, there were extensive relief programmes across Europe. Later, after the Arab–Israeli War of 1948, at the request of the United Nations (UN), Quakers operated relief camps for 250,000 Arab refugees for two years in Gaza. In recognition of their work to relieve famine and suffering during and after both world wars, the Friends Service Council (British) and the American Friends Service Committee were jointly awarded the Nobel Peace Prize in 1947. The chairman of the Nobel Committee, Gunnar Jahn, said:

> It is not the extent of their work or its practical form which is most important. ... It is rather the spirit which animates their work. Theirs is the message of good deeds, the message that men can come into contact with one another in spite of war and in spite of difference of race. May we believe that here there is a hope of laying a foundation for peace among nations, of building up peace in man himself, so that it becomes impossible to settle disputes by the use of force.
>
> (Gunnar Jahn quoted by Yarrow, 1978: pp. 271–272)

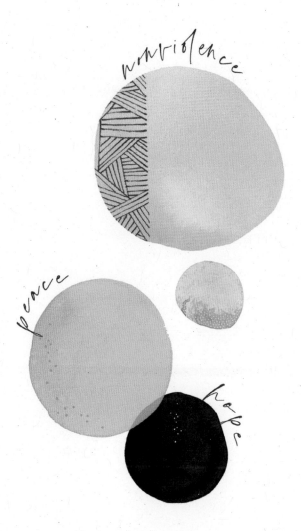

nonviolence

peace

hope

May we believe that here there is a hope of laying a foundation for peace among nations, of building up peace in man himself, so that it becomes impossible to settle disputes by the use of force.

After World War II, alongside the continuance of the relief programmes and Quaker centres, there was a renewed process to build international understanding globally. This included programmes such as International Student Seminars, Seminars in International Affairs and International Work Camps. Another programme, Conferences for Diplomats, grew out of these and had as its focus young diplomats, who would participate in confidential residential meetings spread over several days to discuss issues of national and international significance. Governments were often suspicious of the purposes of the programme, and initially some were reluctant to allow their young diplomats to participate. However, the programme went from strength to strength, and it has been estimated that during the period 1952–1976 about ten per cent of the world's diplomatic community met Quakers and each other at these meetings (Clark, 2012). This opened doors for Quakers almost everywhere in the world, and later conciliation efforts were helped by meetings with senior officials who already knew of the Quakers and their commitment to peace through the Conferences for Diplomats.

The programme was ended in 1976. Subsequently, it was felt that a new generation of diplomats might be approached:

> Quaker Peace & Service attempted to re-start the work in London in 1986 ... and found that *the moment and momentum had passed*; diplomats neither had the time to give in days, nor were they as influential as before.[2] That amazing network of diplomatic connections worldwide has almost disappeared now.
>
> (Andrew Clark, confidential committee
> paper, 2012, original emphasis)

---

2 This programme ran for several years before being laid down in the early 1990s.

The founding of the UN in 1945 led to the creation of Quaker offices in Geneva and New York, which provided opportunities to hold confidential meetings with those involved in issues being discussed at the UN. This work continues, and the format of these meetings is discussed in more detail in chapter 4. Representatives built on their existing connections and developed new ones, working on issues of concern to Quakers worldwide. This form of working was developed with the establishment of Quaker Council for European Affairs (QCEA) in 1979 to work with the European Economic Community, later the European Union, and based at Quaker House in Brussels:

> By creating space … in Quaker Houses in New York, Brussels and Geneva we help shape UN and other international priorities, and we bring attention to issues that are not yet on the international agenda. The reputation and atmosphere of our Quaker Houses allows for the emergence of more reflective and inclusive responses to difficult issues; ideas which might not be heard in more formal settings. The scale of international negotiations can feel challenging, but the trusting environment we provide, informed by Quaker methods, remains key to our work.
>
> (Quaker United Nations Office Geneva, 'How conciliation translates into our work', paper prepared for the Woodbrooke consultation, 2019)

The model was adapted when Quaker House Belfast was established. Staff were able to build on both a history of Quaker relief during the famine and relationships developed during the early days of the 'Troubles'. A quiet, neutral area of Belfast was chosen for Quaker House, and it provided opportunities for off-the-record meetings with politicians, paramilitary representatives, senior civil servants, community leaders and others. This process provided many opportunities for conciliation during the period 1982–2007.

This approach was replicated with the founding of a Quaker Centre (later Friends House) Moscow in 1991, which again built on a lengthy history of involvement with the country and relationships developed since World War II. The appointed representatives worked with conflicts facing society in Russia and neighbouring countries.

Quaker International Affairs Representatives (QIARs) formed another strand among the accumulation of knowledge, contacts, relationship building, and opportunities for Quakers to contribute to peacemaking programmes. They were not based in a Quaker house but had a roving mission that crossed physical borders. There was a QIAR based in Berlin who worked between the two Germanies during the Cold War. Others were based in a region, such as India or Pakistan, the Middle East, or Asia. They built up relationships with members of all sectors of society, developed a deep understanding of the issues that had led to conflict and gained the trust of those with whom they were working. They supported conciliation work in their own regions and provided information for Quaker United Nations Office (QUNO) and other Quakers involved in work in the countries in which they were based. They had flexibility to move freely and to identify areas of need so that they could provide assistance. An example of this arose after the First Gulf War (1990–1991), when the QIARs in the Middle East worked with the main Quaker agencies and led to the appointment of a QIAR to Iraq, based in Baghdad. The purpose of this appointment was to have someone in the country to maintain links with those affected by the war, provide relief and build relationships within society. Their insights into the situation assisted Quaker bodies to focus their work after the conflict.

In 1993, Quaker Peace & Service established a programme called Environmental Intermediaries, drawing on its previous experience and models of working, its knowledge of engaging with decision-makers and -shapers at central and regional levels, and its close links to QUNO and the international community. It focused on major issues facing small farmers in Africa and the impact of dams in India. Its representatives held confidential, off-the-record meetings with politicians, bankers, the UN, and the World Bank, acting as intermediaries "trying to ensure that the voices of experience of Southern farmers relating to access to and benefits from plant genetic resources and intellectual property rights including patents, are heard" (Clark, 2012). Similar work was done in relation to hydropower schemes. Although this work was discontinued in the late 1990s, it formed a strand that informs and continues in Quakers' current work on the environment and the impact of climate change.

Responsibility for the various strands mentioned above was held by the Quaker institutions that provided the staff and resources to manage the work. Within these institutions' structures were Quaker committees with the expertise to oversee the direction of the work and offer professional advice. Links were maintained between the different strands and attempts were made to ensure that confidential work remained out of the public domain.

Those with oversight of all of the work have also had to try to balance, on the one hand, the need to protect the confidentiality of the conciliation work with, on the other hand, the desire of those with a concern for victims of injustice and human rights abuses to speak out, campaign and bring the issues into public view. This is an ongoing dilemma. The inevitable challenge for Quakers who feel led by their commitment to peace, which then engenders action, is the need to weigh up the roles of prophetic Quaker voice and reconciler. They must ensure that campaigns on issues of concern do not impede the conciliation work. Mike Yarrow described this process as accepting:

the fact that there are circumstances when confrontation may be more appropriate than conciliation; circumstances when conciliation, defined as harmonising opposing perspectives, may be entirely inappropriate for goals of human betterment. The two indeed serve quite different purposes: confrontation strives to increase the awareness of latent or patent injustices; conciliation aims to compromise conflicting human goals in some median position that is bound to contain elements of injustice for one side or both. Any given situation may call for agitation and conciliation in different proportions and at different times. The third-party intervenor has to be in touch with the major contending forces at all times, alert to the actualities, and pressing conciliation when appropriate and possible.

(Yarrow, 1978: p. 290)

Although numerically small and without the resources of a large organisation, Quakers have been able to make significant contributions to international conciliation and sustain these for lengthy periods of time. They have built up a network of connections that has helped them to develop a knowledge base, which has in turn enabled them to participate in activities on an international level. In addition to the examples already mentioned, this has included involvement in both South Africa and Zimbabwe, and in relations between the East and West. Furthermore, programmes have brought together ex-combatants from Northern Ireland, Latin America and southern Africa to draw on the participants' accumulation of knowledge and skills. Conciliation work in other areas of the world is ongoing but at the moment remains confidential.

There has been a steady process of building trust and strong relationships through the various programmes, and this has earned opportunities to engage with conciliation programmes because of Quakers' links with many of the people involved. In this way, Quakers have accumulated 'credit', which has (as already outlined) provided openings for future work. However, like all credit, it has to be handled with care and not abused. In time, unless future programmes restore the amount of 'credit' Quakers have available, it will run out.

The world is changing. What was possible in the past may not be so in the future, with the rise of global terrorism, the climate crisis and the fracturing of society now being seen in the UK and elsewhere in the West. At present, Quakers' skills and knowledge enable them to engage with opportunities for international conciliation, but the challenge will be how to continue to lay the groundwork for the future. How can Quakers remain engaged participants rather than observers, passing on the experiences of others rather than their own experiences? How can they hear the genuine voices of those who need to be heard? How and where can they continue to build relationships of trust? Where and what kinds of work should they engage in to enable this to happen in the future? Unless Quakers continue to be engaged with international institutions and accumulate experience of what is happening at local levels regionally, they will have excluded themselves from opportunities for conciliation by default.

The Consultation in International Conciliation held at Woodbrooke in September 2019 addressed these questions, and many of the details are set out in subsequent chapters of this book.

Chapter 2

Principles of Quaker international conciliation

As mentioned in the introduction to this book, conciliation is the process of bringing people together and creating enough trust between them for them to talk constructively together. It usually involves the help of facilitators to encourage the parties to move to that point and to engage in dialogue to resolve the conflict that has divided them.

> The reason Friends can do this sort of work is that we have no power to determine the outcome. We don't make, or even influence, international opinion or decisions of support or indeed of penalising the player. It is only the relationship that we build that influences those who decide.
>
> (Bob Neidhardt, unpublished committee paper, 1995)

The Quaker spiritual base

A belief in the concept that there is 'that of God in everyone' has led Quakers, since very early in their history, to take the position that to engage in violent conflict is inconsistent with their beliefs. This finds its logical expression in the belief that there are innate qualities of goodness in everyone, even if they are not easily visible. It was expressed by Sue Williams as follows:

> There is something of God in everyone, therefore we oppose killing. Paradoxically, there is also something of God in people who kill or use violence, so we also oppose killing them. We are motivated not by partisan or commercial aims, but by transcendent values: pacifism, nonviolence, balanced partiality. All of this must be visible in our actions over time. Words will not be convincing.

- A Sri Lankan politician: "I trust you as mediator because you want an outcome which is fair and less destructive, and you don't have a preferred option."
- An IRA spokesman: "You're the only people I talk with who don't necessarily agree with me, but don't want me dead."

(Sue Williams, paper prepared for
the Woodbrooke consultation, 2019)

This belief involves respect for everyone and accepting people as they are, but it does not mean that Quakers are uncritical or naive. Quakers have developed testimonies that are expressions of their faith that lead to action. There are testimonies to equality, truth and integrity, simplicity, peace, and more recently an awareness of a need to care for the earth and the environment – all of which underpin Quaker thought and practice. Since the early days of Quakerism, the commitment to the testimony to peace has had implications at both personal and institutional levels, and the Society of Friends is one of the historical Peace Churches.

This spiritual grounding has formed the bedrock of Quakers' work and has been seen as the expression of their faith in action. Quakers have a shared sense of values and a vision based on their testimonies, which has enabled them to engage with a wide range of people and situations. Quakers' belief that there is 'that of God in everyone' leads to respect and an understanding of the importance of walking alongside them. It helps Quakers to accept others as they are and to recognise the challenges they are facing. In valuing each individual, Quakers attempt to hear all voices, giving time and thought to the process. Where there is suffering, this should be recognised and any legitimate grievances need to be dealt with within the process. The testimony to simplicity leads to Quakers seeing their role as enabling, not seeking any recognition of their own part in the process but instead allowing themselves to be used as a channel and helping the process to take place. This is challenging but essential. This spiritual underpinning and the process of conciliation do not exist in isolation but form part of Quakers' wider witness and draw on resources, both human and organisational. As a result, we need to question and review the impact of every situation with which we are involved in order to extract good practice, take the lesson and assess its ongoing usefulness.

> Perhaps the most distinctive element of the Quaker approach has been patience and commitment. … At its best, this patience is not just stubbornness. Nor is it a naive optimism not grounded in political realities. Neither of these attitudes will be of much value to those directly involved in the conflict. Rather, it is an outward manifestation of a confidence that situations can improve, and that individuals have the potential to change and take initiatives which can open up new ways forward. It is a recognition of the potential of the individual and the power of a force which is not governed by material or selfish considerations. By their very presence, they can convey the belief that human relations do not have to be as they are, and the belief in people's capacity to make a difference.
>
> (Clem McCartney and Sue Williams, 'Distinctive elements of Quaker mediation', unpublished paper, 1997)

In focusing on the spiritual roots of Quaker involvement in international conciliation, it is also important to remember that those with whom we work will have their own principles. It is easy to stereotype the members of armed groups, some of whom may not fit our preconceived images. Some will share principles (perhaps based in faith) that we recognise, while with others there will be a struggle to find common ground. Developing a shared understanding of guiding principles, a common language to express them and a commitment to respect for those with whom we work is part of the process. Quakers have, at times, found themselves earnestly praying alongside people who have used weapons and killed. The beliefs and experiences that have led to those individuals' decisions to engage in violent conflict in order to gain their declared goals are fundamental parts of who they are and their hopes for future outcomes.

A letter of thanks from a senior member of an armed group expressed its members' feelings at a crucial stage of the conciliation process:

> More intensive dialogues will continue. On behalf of the leadership and all ranks and files both from Civil and … Army and general Public … and on my behalf, convey our warmest Congratulations and heartfelt gratitude to you and the Quaker team as because of your selfless and tireless efforts [we] can now live in absolute peace with the freedom to go to any part of the World to acknowledge the Almighty God, including the visits to Quakers, London.

> God Bless. Thank you once again. With warmest wishes.

Principles of conciliation as set out by the Quaker Peace & Social Witness Conciliation Group

The Quaker Peace & Social Witness (QPSW) Conciliation Group has set out five principles of conciliation, as follows:

A. Not taking sides but recognising the suffering of everyone.

B. Encouraging exploration to discover nonviolent responses at all times.

C. Seeking to build the capacity of local peaceworkers and peace groups.

D. Strict confidentiality of conversation and dialogue.

E. Being transparent and open.

Many, if not all, of these basic principles are actually applicable across all Quaker social action. They are applied in various types of work, but the principles remain the same. The remainder of this chapter explores each of these principles in detail and how they are applied to processes of conciliation.

A. Not taking sides but recognising the suffering of everyone

This principle includes six concepts.

Not taking sides

While not taking sides in any conciliation processes with which we are involved, we are not coming from a position of neutrality. Our commitment to peace is part of our witness to the sanctity of life as expressed through our testimonies and belief that there is 'that of God in everyone'. However, we are also aware that in this process, we are working from a position of principled impartiality.

Engaging in conciliation involves working with individuals and groups who have promoted violence to achieve their goals. It means working with people who have very different views in order to gain a deeper understanding of their aims, while maintaining a strong moral but neutral position ourselves. For example, it involves not

Engaging in conciliation means working with people who have very different views in order to gain a deeper understanding of their aims, while maintaining a strong moral but neutral position ourselves.

allowing groups to be talked out of their human rights while, at the same time, not compromising our own principles by allowing conversations to drift into justification of things that are contrary to human rights.

QPSW has addressed this with helpful guidelines that refer to principled impartiality:

> Principled impartiality is seen as a benchmark of acceptable standards based on international standards, especially at a time when what we might regard as moral behaviour is being disregarded and eroded.
>
> (Confidential QPSW document)

Building relationships of trust

> The world of disputes and conflict is difficult and hostile and does not value open and trusting relationships. People are often driven by personal interests or the interests of their institutions and organisations, which they may feel are under threat. This seems to give them permission to be deceitful and manipulative, or forceful and bullying, in ways they would not condone in other circumstances or at other times.
>
> In these situations, it is even more important to offer personal connections based on confidence and trust. There can be something very powerful in not having power and yet being open and trusting, but not naive. We need to be "wise as serpents and gentle as doves" and having the personal confidence to be innocent and vulnerable, makes this easier.
>
> (Clem McCartney, 'Reflections on Quaker involvement in conciliation', paper prepared for the Woodbrooke consultation, 2019)

'Parachuting' conciliators into a situation, without initial trust-building, will not assist the process. The early stages of trust-building are time consuming and often initiated by those asking for Quakers' involvement, having had previous contact with their work. This may have been Quakers' commitment to peace, engagement in conciliation with similar situations, or work in relieving humanitarian need at a local level or with international institutions such as the United Nations. Whatever the initial links, building trust is an extremely slow process that cannot be hurried. It comes from a willingness to walk with others, be ready to talk with everyone and engage with the issues. It has to start with where others are. The would-be conciliators are tested for reliability, awareness of the complexities of the situation, impartiality and so on, and only after their credentials in these areas have been recognised does the relationship develop.

The initial trust is built with individuals, by being ready to go at their pace and not trying to hurry the process. It takes time to overcome suspicion and develop these relationships, especially with those in leadership positions, who may feel isolated and physically vulnerable in spite of their public personas. Most of those engaging in the process are under considerable stress, which adds to their sense of anxiety when developing new relationships of trust. Not only are they challenged by the external conflict but there may also be challenges within their own group. Trust in conciliators may not be something they find easy to build. Additionally, although trust may be developed with some of the group, others may not feel the same level of confidence in what is happening, so different forces may work to both support and undermine the trust-building process. Even when trust has been established, it will be tested from time to time. Typically, those with whom conciliators work have had considerable experience of trust and promises being broken.

Once built, the relationship of trust can be transferred to others in the conciliation team but not without reservations. With each change in the team, a measure of trust may be transferred, but the remainder has to be re-earned and no short cuts or assumptions should be made.

Any conciliators trying to develop relationships of trust need to take into account the political, economic, social, and cultural environment in which they are working. This requires sensitivity and a willingness to be open to bearing all of these factors in mind when developing relationships. It is vital to put personal views of the world to one side, be ready to 'hear' what is being said, and not try to superimpose one's own perceptions when attempting to interpret the experience of others.

The aim is to build a sustainable relationship of trust that can form the basis of shared work, but this is not a friendship. Objectivity and impartiality have to remain at the core of the relationship. Any 'drift' into friendship will undermine the process.

Listening

It is crucial to listen to each side's story, however many times it needs to be told. This involves active listening, which means engaging with the stories that are told while remaining objective and not being drawn into one more than another. Stories can become repetitive and listeners can easily dismiss this part of the process as unnecessary. However, when Quakers were working with various people involved in the 'Troubles' in Northern Ireland, each new contact began with their own lengthy description of the violence, its causes and its outcomes as perceived by the speaker. This was an important part of the process because each individual needed to express their sense of what had happened and how it had influenced

If each person's (or their side's) grievances and history are not 'heard' and acknowledged, it is difficult to move forward.

them and their (or their side's) position. It was about setting down a marker – setting out the context of the person's (or their side's) grievances and history, and why they were where they were. If this had not been 'heard' and acknowledged, it would have been difficult to move forward.

Being a good listener – accurately remembering what is said and being able to interpret what others are saying – forms one of the building blocks in the conciliation process:

> The discipline includes listening to long histories of suffering and grievance which, though very partisan, are also very real. Eventually, all the grievances on all sides will have to be acknowledged and addressed, which is usually an incremental process, tacking back and forth between justice and security, between language rights and land rights, etc. They will need to come to see the process as being in the interest of their groups and offering some possibility of a settlement. And they will need to see, in action, that the groups they don't trust are willing and able to change somewhat and accept hard truths and imperfect solutions.
>
> (Sue Williams, paper prepared for
> the Woodbrooke consultation, 2019)

Empathy and concern for all caught up in the conflict

Everyone caught up in a conflict has had the experience of their own (or their side's) losses or grievance not being 'heard'. People are often angry about their own sense of injustice, and rightful revenge may seem to be their only option. They have experienced pain and loss and want others to feel their pain. Their own experiences often mean that they are unable to 'hear' the stories of their opponents, and their knowledge of the needs of others may be distorted or inaccurate. They may also be so focused on their own loss that they do not see the consequences of their actions because they have lost sight of the bigger picture.

As indicated above, active listening is essential. This takes time and energy because it is part of the process. It involves conveying empathy and concern for everyone caught up in the conflict without being drawn into the conflict itself.

One danger for outsiders is that although we may wish to walk alongside those with whom we are working, our experience is never theirs. Pity and sympathy are inappropriate, but to convey empathy we have to try to build on our own life experiences to help make the connections. In one conversation I had, a woman from Bosnia and Herzegovina talked of her experiences. Her father and brother had been killed and buried in a mass grave. The desire of the woman and her mother had been to give them a proper funeral, but this was only possible when the mass grave was uncovered. The men were identified by items of their clothing. The woman's sense of loss was overwhelming. In reaching out to her, I was aware that my own life experience of loss was quite different from hers. Saying 'I understand' would have sounded hollow, but I had been to the area – I had met with other women who had experienced similar loss and talked about their emotional distress, and I had also spoken with those who had helped to excavate mass graves. My life experiences were different, but I was able to use and convey my understanding of the woman's grief and reach out to her.

Asking questions

Similar to active listening, the use of non-confrontational questioning is important. An understanding of the participants' needs and wants has to be established early on in the process, and perceptions must be checked and re-checked. Skilful use of questions helps those involved to develop an awareness of their fear of the other. It is important for everybody to realise that they may have a clear understanding of the suffering of their own side, but they are likely to perceive others in a dehumanised fashion. As Clem McCartney described:

> Our own experience of needing help shows us that it is not very helpful to be told that our assessment of the situation is wrong or to be told what we should think and do. We have to work that out for ourselves. The best way to help in that process is to be asked questions in a way that encourages us to test what we think we know and believe and sheds a light on the limitations of our understanding. Supplementary questions that ask 'why …' do that:
>
> • Why does the situation seem like that for you?
> • Why do you assume that others hold the views that you attribute to them? Have you any evidence?
> • Why would they do what you think they will do?
> • Why can you not try a different approach? What would happen if you did?
>
> (Clem McCartney, paper prepared for the Woodbrooke consultation, 2019)

Presenting other options and using questions to explore opportunities helps to widen perspectives. In this way, eventually each group may gain a better understanding of themselves and the other side, and know the impact of their own actions. It is through listening and questioning that it is possible to identify different ways in which both sides might be able to respond to confidence-building initiatives.

Facilitating meetings that are off the record or that serve as seminars for community representatives

It is important to facilitate off-the-record meetings that provide opportunities for discussion and enable the participants to explore joint concerns in a neutral setting. Such meetings provide opportunities for participants to express and 'hear' the needs of everyone. They also provide safe, neutral spaces for groups to explore what they might provide as signals to the other side that they are serious about resolving the conflict.

The planning of such meetings requires time, patience, flexibility, and the ability to go forward when the time seems rights. It is essential to secure an appropriate venue, engage all participants, let everyone know who the other participants will be, prepare a suitable programme, and clearly outline the purpose of the meeting. Such meetings can be cancelled by any one of the participants at the last minute, sometimes for no apparent reason, but the role of the conciliator is to renew efforts and continue the work.

B. Encouraging exploration to discover nonviolent responses at all times

Those involved in armed struggles may already have made a commitment to violent solutions being the way forward. They may feel that the path they have chosen will bring them the victory they desire, and any suggestions of alternative, nonviolent responses may be approached with caution:

> Encourage exploration of nonviolent responses: Yes, and also less violent options. What options did you consider?

What options did your opponents consider when they decided on that course of action? At local as well as national and international levels, it can become possible for parties to identify some of the alternatives each side considers. For example: Your group was offended by the public playing of music to incite you? Perhaps the opponents debated whether to resort to actual violence, destruction of property, nasty graffiti on walls, and ended up deciding on music. In Northern Ireland, long-term processes led informal as well as formal representatives to meet privately to raise grievances, rather than doing so publicly. The mediation process developed the capacity of all parties to interpret actions, to reciprocate in actions, and in that way to work toward communicating directly with words.

(Sue Williams, paper prepared for
the Woodbrooke consultation, 2019)

If they pull back and come to realise that they will be unable to 'win' by violence, the groups are faced with dilemmas. They are often still heavily armed. They will be nervous, fearful of others taking advantage and wanting to keep their options open. Also, if the process is not dealt with skilfully, there may be a residue of violent aggression that can be destructive in the future, as has been seen with the re-emergence of armed factions following their perception that unresolved grievances remain.

The role of conciliators is to try to use established relationships to bring alternative, nonviolent options into the discussions, in this way providing the opposing groups with opportunities to explore alternatives.

The role of conciliators is to try to use established relationships to bring alternative, nonviolent options into the discussions, in this way providing the opposing groups with opportunities to explore alternatives.

C. Seeking to build the capacity of local peaceworkers and peace groups

The reality is that, in really dangerous situations, local people do the vast majority of the peace work, and they understand the situation much better than an incomer will, even if from a partisan perspective. Assuming that you can build their capacity is quite patronising. But it is incredibly inspiring to work collegially, alongside local people, learn from them, and share what you may have learned in other places. Sometimes, you may hold up a mirror, to frame the things they are doing that they haven't identified or systematised. If travel is easier for you than for local people, as it was in Uganda during the civil war, one role is to connect organisations to others they don't know about and take staff to meet each other. At the worst of times, when no one could do anything, we would encourage local peace workers to talk about what they would do when they had a chance to do something, and even do some planning for it. It is hard to be patient when you can't even work toward your goals.

(Sue Williams, paper prepared for
the Woodbrooke consultation, 2019)

During the conflict in the Balkans, Quakers built up strong links with individual peaceworkers and organisations working for peace in Bosnia and Herzegovina, Croatia, and Serbia. These links were formed in response to those individuals' and organisations' requests for assistance and maintained in various ways: visits, grants to organisations wanting to organise gatherings, provision of training programmes run by people with skills developed in other conflict situations, placement of volunteers in nascent peace organisations, and provision of ongoing support for individuals working in difficult situations where they were minority voices. This commitment to them and their work during the conflict formed the basis for future efforts, after the conflict, when Quaker representatives worked with all communities with the aim of building a sustainable peace.

D. Strict confidentiality of conversation and dialogue

Strict confidentiality is at the core of the conciliation process but it raises a number of dilemmas for everyone involved. For example, how should the information be given, received, heard, shared, and recorded? Is the information being shared in confidence with the intention of forwarding the process, to check on the reliability of the conciliators or for some other purpose? It is part of the role of those involved in conciliation processes to check what is being said or heard and to handle it with care. Sometimes the commitment to confidentiality is challenged by dilemmas – for example, whom should be trusted? What should be done with the information and should it be shared? There is also the need to keep some record of meetings to help the team to stand back and analyse the processes. Supporting committees and individuals will want updates. Another challenge for the conciliators is how much to share while protecting the confidentiality of the individuals and groups involved in the process. The preparation of any report, for any purpose, brings with it questions around confidentiality, and it must be anticipated who will read it and how they may deal with the information.

Alongside the dilemmas around sharing confidential information with committees, there are challenges relating to sharing confidential information within the wider organisation. The sensitive work of international conciliation may at times come into conflict with activities being carried out by other parts of the wider organisation that are engaged with public protests. Or there may be a perceived need to make public statements on situations of ongoing conflict, which could impact on the work of the international conciliation team. Any such statement requires care and sensitive wording, but there can often be unexpected outcomes. Mike Yarrow described such a process and its consequences:

> The Quaker publication *Search for Peace in the Middle East*[3] ... was directed mainly toward the American public, because of the special relations between the United States and Israel. ... It was a balanced statement worked over carefully through more than fifteen revisions, discussed at each stage with Arab and Israeli spokesmen, but this did not forestall the storm of protest that came, particularly from Israeli officials and American Jewish organizations who felt that the Quakers' 'even-handed' approach was against them. The results had both positive and negative influences on the total conciliation effort of the Quakers, and it is too early to tell whether it was wise to publish it or not, for the conflict and Quaker efforts continue.
>
> (Yarrow, 1978: pp. 276–277)

However, in spite of these dilemmas, the commitment to confidentiality is essential:

> Confidentiality: If we are talking to people on different sides of a dispute, we can become aware of misunderstandings that maintain the conflict, but how can we provide the information that will clarify the misunderstanding if we have received it in confidence? Nevertheless, insights derived from those discussions can be used to raise questions which help the interlocutor to speculate on what other parties really think or want and why they are talking or behaving the way they do.
>
> (Clem McCartney, paper prepared for the Woodbrooke consultation, 2019)

---

3   American Friends Service Committee (1970).

E. Being transparent and open

The final principle was concisely summed up in Sue Williams' paper for the consultation. She said that conciliators should be transparent and open but "with limitations":

> If conciliators are working only with one group, it can be possible to be fully transparent. But mediators who work with and between a number of groups will always have to balance openness with confidentiality. When you meet with people and assure them that you will not pass on confidential information, they will test whether you do. And, if they see that you are willing to bring them confidential information from their opponents, they will (and should) assume that you are giving their confidences to the opponents. It is important to be honest, but it is not always possible to be transparent. There are, in a way, two rules of thumb: Do not say to any party what you would not like to have known publicly and try not to have anything known publicly. You cannot control whether people you meet with release information themselves, nor whether journalists publish things. In Uganda at that time [1980s], it was too dangerous for any journalists to be there seeking 'scoops'. In Northern Ireland, most journalists were, as we were ourselves, resident there, and wanted peace more than they wanted a scoop. Elsewhere, by contrast, our limited experience was of media very willing to destroy a peace initiative for a story. These kinds of variations reinforce the importance of bouncing ideas off knowledgeable local people, perhaps in the form of a reference group.
>
> (Sue Williams, paper prepared for
> the Woodbrooke consultation, 2019)

Closing thoughts on the principles

The five principles, as set out above in some detail, are not used by Quakers alone but form the approach of many others involved with conciliation, both secular and from other faith groups. The following extract provides an example of all five principles in action. It recounts an interfaith process – including Quakers – that emphasised the inclusion of women's voices and the importance of 'insider' mediators in a conciliation process:

> We ... have more acute understandings that many contemporary peace processes (according to the specific conflict dynamics) begin within small groups and communities who can exert change amid divided societies. There has also been a growing recognition of the importance of 'insider' mediators.
>
> Indonesia was another unitary state dominated by a powerful man and military which underwent a huge transition ('tranformasi') when Suharto stood down in 1998. It was there that I had the privilege of working in a backstop and support capacity for a small team of Indonesian mediators who went from Java to assist in another island communal conflict (location: the Moluccas). I tell this because of my belief that what we name as Quaker principles of mediation and conciliation are also often qualities which those of other faiths and persuasions possess and that it is vital that we recognise, reach out and work collaboratively. Examples include trust, continuity and relationship building, seeing that of God in the other, discretion (keeping a low profile) and long-term commitment.

In the case from the Moluccas, long-simmering inequalities, deprivation, economic exploitation and lack of political representation exploded in a form which took on blame and identity mobilisation between Christians and Muslims. There were three individuals, two men and one woman, who took it upon themselves to intervene on the ground for grassroots and community. The woman took the lead in crossing a literal 'line' in the capital city and island territory. She was herself from a long-respected and devout Muslim family on Java. For her work as a go-between and conciliator she took off her hijab, to demonstrate to the Christian 'side' that she was not aligned only to one group but to the humanity in all islanders. She lived all of the qualities as mentioned above, as well as humility and acute listening skills. Eventually, through building trust and dedicated honest brokering, she was able to bring the opposing parties to a place where they agreed to interact in the search for a common solution. This was not a simple process but a significant achievement along the way[4] to a peaceful outcome. Later these same three individuals began a centre for security and peace which became prominent in an Indonesian university, with capacity to assist in other regions. And I keep in touch with the woman mediator, who has become a close friend over many years of shared concerns and working in partnership.

(Judith Large, paper prepared for
the Woodbrooke consultation, 2019)

---

4   Judith Large and Clem McCartney assisted the three Indonesian mediators in a subsequent large-group intervention that facilitated cross-community, interfaith and multi-generational dialogue within this particular conflict. The results were positive.

nonviolence

hope

courage

Chapter 3

What have we learnt?

As indicated in chapter 1, Quakers have a long history of involvement in international conciliation. Learning has been shared, and over the generations a body of knowledge has been gathered. Academic institutions and other organisations, both faith-based and secular, have also drawn on the learning from Quakers' experiences and, as a result, there is now considerable material available for all involved in this field of work.

Quaker international conciliators have reflected on this wide range of experience. Attempts to evaluate and analyse previous Quaker experience have enabled conciliators to build on the past and inform future action. This chapter explores this learning in more detail, building on the principles set out in chapter 2, which were:

A. Not taking sides but recognising the suffering of everyone.
B. Encouraging exploration to discover nonviolent responses at all times.
C. Seeking to build the capacity of local peaceworkers and peace groups.
D. Strict confidentiality of conversation and dialogue.
E. Being transparent and open.

Stages of the peace process and where conciliation fits in

Those outside the peace process often express confusion about the use of the terminology 'peacemaking', 'peacekeeping' and 'peacebuilding'. They are often aware that there are differences between these stages but unsure as to what exactly those differences are. The terms can be defined as follows:

- **Peacemaking** is the process of trying to find a way to end a violent conflict via an agreement that is acceptable to all parties. This may include political, diplomatic or military intervention and takes different forms according to the situation.
- **Peacekeeping** is intended to ensure that the agreement is monitored. It involves monitoring local activity and being ready to use force if necessary.
- **Peacebuilding** includes a range of activities, such as working with those involved in the conflict at many levels, and addressing their concerns and grievances in order to build a sustainable peace.

Quaker activity has concentrated on two of the three stages: peacemaking and peacebuilding.

Peacemaking

Peacemaking (the focus of this book) has occurred in many regions of the world. It involves working with all involved in a violent conflict, including national and local leaders, military and paramilitary personnel, faith leaders and civilian leaders – essentially, anyone with influence who is able to assist the process of bringing about a peaceful resolution to the violent conflict.

Peacemaking depends on building relationships at all levels in society. It requires caring for those relationships with no idea of whether or not they will eventually contribute to the process. Relationship building takes time, patience and a commitment to finding a sustainable peace. It requires those involved to be ready to respond to requests for assistance. This can be challenging, especially in the conciliation process, when, during the peacemaking stage, those trying to assist must aim to be available whenever an opportunity arises. This may involve lengthy flights, meetings that

suffering

fear

assumptions

Peacemaking depends on building relationships at all levels in society.
It requires caring for those relationships with no idea of whether
or not they will eventually contribute to the process.

are aborted at the last minute and a readiness to remain up to date with local developments, whether or not the opportunity to put this knowledge into use ever arises. It means recognising the possibility that the situation may deteriorate and that those involved may feel that the only way forward is violent conflict. It requires a state of readiness and commitment to the peacemaking process in both individuals and organisations, and it is accompanied by physical, financial and organisational demands.

Sometimes those involved maintain their links from a distance, undertaking planned visits as appropriate, and on other occasions the conciliators are based within the country concerned. Sue Williams has provided an example of the latter:

> As Quaker representatives, Steve [Williams] and I learned what a great gift autonomy is. When we agreed to go to Uganda in 1984, the brief we were given by QPS [Quaker Peace & Service] was essentially: We think there is a war on in Uganda. Go and see what you can do.
>
> We were in our thirties, with various degrees and experiences, but this certainly looked like a challenge. Members of our committee in London gave us various suggestions (some of them *very* firmly stated) of what they thought we should do, and we had all this in mind. But, once arrived in Kampala, we simply began by asking everyone we met: Who is doing something that might promote peace or reconciliation? When a group or individual was mentioned several times, we would seek them out, learn more about what they were doing, and ask: How can we help? We had the autonomy to build our work on the basis of what we found and learned in Uganda, and in collaboration with inspiring people. Some of the shuttle mediation with rebel groups we did on our own,

at least to begin with. But QPS gave us the space to ask, to learn, and to try to find ways to help build peace. I think that experience of autonomy laid the foundation for the way we would work over the next decades.

(Sue Williams, paper prepared for
the Woodbrooke consultation, 2019)

Peacebuilding

The same skills are used in peacebuilding, which focuses on helping with confidence-building programmes, capacity-building programmes and training opportunities after an agreement has been reached. This has involved Quakers working with local peace groups, community decision-makers and decision-shapers; helping to build cross-community dialogue; addressing the grievances and injustices that led to the original conflict; and exploring opportunities for reconciliation.

An example of this occurred in Croatia in 2005, when the Quaker representative Goran Božičević, having identified war veterans as the area on which to focus, worked with a number of organisations to develop a programme. Initially, he concentrated on those he referred to as 'soft' war veterans, but gradually he recognised that for the work to deepen, he needed to attract 'hardliners'. He realised that he needed to adjust his language to use the language of the veterans, such as 'homeland war'. This attracted a wider range of participants at his seminars, including some who were prepared to explore a range of sensitive issues. Many of the participants were sceptical, but they usually remained and engaged in challenging discussions:

The focus of this programme with war veterans was in time extended to include human rights activists and organisations representing victims. ... A retired major of the Croatian Army wrote to Božičević:

"I came by coincidence but also out of curiosity. We were surprised looking at the list of invitees, so we decided to come, ready to leave the very first day if we didn't like it. After four days of discussions ('struggle' would be a more appropriate word) between 'us' and 'them' I returned home, to my sincere amazement empowered and, in a way, transformed. For the first time after the war, having such an opportunity, I realised that former enemies can talk with one another and even more than that need to. I realised that talk, in my case, helps to better understand myself and the other one. I was surprised with the level of tolerance and dialogue. Although we had completely opposite opinions about the causes and consequences of the war, we were listening to and even hearing (!) the arguments of the other side. And they were listening to our arguments. There I learnt about the importance of facilitators and the skills and knowledge needed."

(Bennett, 2015: pp. 24–25)

When to become involved

Given the physical, financial and organisational commitment required during involvement in a conciliation process, it is important to ensure that becoming involved is not taken lightly. Requests may be made for Quaker assistance, based on Quakers' reputation in other violent conflicts, but any such request should not be pursued without extensive thought about what it would entail and the organisation's capacity to respond.

A useful 'traffic-light tool' has been developed for use at this stage by the charitable organisation Responding to Conflict (RTC). The following has been adapted from the book *Working with conflict: Skills and strategies for action*, written by RTC practitioners (Fisher et al., 2000).

Stop

Think before starting. Undertake a full analysis of the situation using all available tools. What is involved? Questions need to be addressed before proceeding. For example:

- Have Quakers had involvement with the area and/or those involved in the conflict?
- Is Quakers' previous work in the area likely to help or hinder the process?
- Would you be perceived as impartial?
- Do you have sufficient knowledge of the politics and the social and cultural issues of the region to play a part in the process?
- Has the request for assistance come from one or several of those involved in the conflict, and are most of them happy for you to become involved?
- Does the request have the support of any Quakers in the region?
- Are there people from the area who might fulfil this role? If not, is there a clear role for you that would enable them to contribute to the process?
- Who would benefit from Quakers' involvement?

Look

Consider the following questions:

- Has an analysis of the conflict and possible ways forward been explored?
- Are there Quakers with experience of conciliation and of the region who might be available to do the work?
- Would those directly involved with the conciliation have the time and energy to undertake the necessary background reading and develop a detailed knowledge of the situation and its history? Would they be free to not only attend meetings to develop the strategic thinking but also travel to the area of conflict?
- Is the team sustainable? Does the organisation have the capacity to sustain the process?
- What would be the cost (in terms of time and resources as well as money) of supporting this work, and what impact would it have on options to develop other work? Given that we are living in a world of finite resources, what would need to change?

Listen

No situation exists in a vacuum and others will already be involved. Ensure that you listen to them and ensure that others feel that you have something special to contribute. Consider the following:

- If there are local Quakers in the region, what is their opinion and how could your involvement in the conciliation process impinge on them and their witness?

- How would you know the best time to become involved and take initiatives?
- Is this the right time to become involved?

Proceed

Conciliation work is a huge commitment and the decision to proceed should not be taken lightly. It should also be recognised that most of the work is likely to be undertaken by people from the region. Before making the decision to fly in an international team, it is important to take time to ask these and related questions.

(Adapted from Fisher et al., 2000: pp. 14–15)

Determining when and where to start is not always easy. Sue Williams commented:

When? The earlier the better. It is always more difficult once people have been killed. Non-lethal violence, even latent violence, is an appropriate reason for intervention. The history of Quaker intervention is primarily a combination of very long-term mediation initiatives (at one time, the average length of involvement of Quakers was 12 years) and what in the Jordans document[5] are called 'missions'. The latter implies that intervenors come into a situation for a limited time. There are also examples of Quaker mediators being involved in a situation repeatedly over the years, without being in residence (such as Everett Mendelsohn in the Middle

---

5   The report that followed the 1989 conference (see Introduction).

East). My own experience under the auspices of Quakers is primarily of long-term, residential involvement. Under other auspices, I have been engaged in a number of situations for a short time, sometimes repeatedly.

(Sue Williams, paper prepared for the Woodbrooke consultation, 2019)

Jonathan Woolley, Director of Quaker United Nations Office (QUNO) Geneva, spoke at the Woodbrooke consultation about the office's opportunities for work on climate change. He gave an example of how QUNO Geneva had applied the traffic-light model to determine how, where and when to work. The office had the contacts, experience and conciliation skills to assist with a process at the United Nations (UN) that is of concern among Quakers, but it is an overpopulated field with many governments and organisations heavily involved and there was no obvious entry point for QUNO Geneva. However, Woolley said, "We kept hearing that people involved in the process didn't know each other, which led to a small space for Quaker work." After much thought and preparation, QUNO Geneva held its first meeting for some of those involved in the UN discussions about climate change, bringing together people who needed to be prepared for working in this specialised area. Many of the diplomats felt hemmed in by the briefs they had received from their governments, and the meeting provided a safe space in which to discuss options for ways forward. It started with a meal, and a process was started through building trust and personal connections. The Quakers came to the first meeting with 'hearts and minds prepared' and ready for whatever might open up.

So far, 19 dinners and lunches on climate change have been held. QUNO Geneva's role is to listen and encourage – not to promote a particular view but to provide solidarity and support for the negotiators.

Developing the team

Having explored the request for involvement in an international conciliation process, undertaken an analysis of the situation, and considered the possibility that Quakers might have the knowledge and skills to contribute, the next stage is to develop the team. It is difficult to undertake this type of work in isolation, and over the years we have learnt much about how to bring together a group of Quakers who will work together closely over a period of time. Much of this experience has been drawn from when the constituent parts worked and when they didn't! Learning has been brought from our understanding of the theory and practice of group work, and its members have built up a body of knowledge over the years. Given the uncertainty over whether or not a specific conciliation process will even start, let alone function over a period of time, there has to be considerable flexibility among the team. Members must also be prepared to achieve very little even if considerable effort is put into the early stages.

The aim is to bring together a team that has the capacity to work together, sometimes in challenging circumstances and in periods of intense activity. The individuals within the team need to have an understanding of who they are, emotional intelligence, and a sense of security within themselves before engaging with others. The team should be made up of individuals who have had some experience of living in other cultures and thereby developing sensitivity to the lives of those around them. It is possible to live in a different culture yet be unaware of the political, social and economic challenges faced by local people – or to be aware but only be able to see these challenges through the critical lens of an outsider. It is almost impossible to become completely detached from our own culture, but there is a need for those involved in international conciliation to be able to develop sensitivity to and empathy for those with whom they work.

They are not the 'other' but fellow human beings with needs to be understood and respected. Additionally, some experience of living in violent situations can provide preparation for what the team might hear or see, as well as an awareness of the impact that violent conflict has on those living in such a situation.

While recognising and developing an understanding of the cultural patterns of the situation, it is also important to be aware of the 'baggage' we bring with us from our own culture. We may be aware of the disadvantages that come from people's perceptions of us as (for example) white, male and from a country with a colonial past. However, we may miss the need to be sensitive in our use of language and may inadvertently indicate that we are supporting one 'side' and unable to be neutral. Examples include the use of certain names of towns or regions (such as the varying underlying impressions conveyed by using 'Londonderry' versus 'Derry' in Northern Ireland) and the use of different forms of pronunciation. It takes time to learn how to deal with these issues. No one is ever completely neutral, but an awareness that 'baggage' exists is essential when assembling a team.

The team needs to reflect the skills required to do the work (see more on this below), but it is also necessary to consider how the attributes of the team are balanced, especially in relation to the cultural expectations of those with whom the team will be working. For example, a Quaker may wish to assemble a team that is balanced in terms of gender, age and ethnicity, but it has to be recognised that the presence of (for example) younger participants or women may have either a positive or a negative impact on those with whom they will be working. This is especially relevant when engaging with traditional patriarchal societies, which tend to revere those who have reached old age. Awareness of potential impact is needed, although it may not prevent the selection of specific team members.

memory

assumptions

beliefs

"…it is also important to be aware of the 'baggage'
we bring with us from our own culture."

A useful comment came from one of the small group discussions at the Woodbrooke consultation:

> Our conciliation work is done by volunteers, not professionals. But we realise this is only possible because of our privilege – we are rich in comparison to those we want to help. This can limit the diversity within our teams.
>
> (Participant comment, Woodbrooke consultation, 2019)

Recognition of the dynamics within a group and an ability to understand how teams work together – both positively and negatively – are vital. A number of roles will evolve within the group, in order to enable it to function effectively, but it is essential that energy is focused on the conciliation process, with none being diverted into power struggles within the team. There will be differences of opinion, but it is essential that all members of the team understand group dynamics and are able to function within a team setting. Once formed, the team will develop its own ways of working, sharing confidential information and keeping records. The relationships within a team are based on trust and take time to evolve, but previous experience of working in this way will speed the process of team-building.

From time to time, people will leave because it is not always possible for them to give long periods of service. Conversely, too, if individuals remain for too long, this may limit the creativity of the team and its willingness to explore fresh avenues. New members will likely replace them as the team will need to be strengthened, and this may introduce skills or knowledge not held by existing members. These new members will have to be integrated into the working of the team, and this will test its flexibility. At the same time, there is a need for stability within the team because its purpose is to build relationships of trust with those involved in the violent conflict. A fine balance is needed.

Along with the need to consider stability and interchangeability within the team, there is a need to consider its size. The pool of potential members needs to be large enough to do the work, but not everyone will be able to travel when the need arises. Individuals within the team need the flexibility in their personal lives to be available to undertake the necessary preparation and keep up to date with the changing situation. It is voluntary work and requires a long-term commitment. In the past, employers were able to release members of staff to undertake this type of work, but changing work patterns mean that this is no longer as viable. One consequence is that the pool of potential team members is often made up of those who are retired. They have more flexibility, but they may also have family responsibilities and a higher likelihood of health issues.

Finally, in addition to the team members, a person is needed to act in an administrative capacity. This person may or may not be part of the travelling team.

The overall aim is to build a strong, diverse group that has the capacity to work together to achieve a common purpose. Time will be required to bond and build trust but also to do all the background reading required – before and during the team's term of service. Many situations are swift moving, so it is essential that team members have frequent updates and an understanding of developments in the region. Additionally, the conciliation process requires team members to maintain links with governments and their relevant departments, the country's diaspora and the Foreign & Commonwealth Office.

Central to any Quaker team involved in international conciliation is a shared perception of the spiritual dimension of the work. A Quaker team has shared values that underpin the way in which its members work together. Opportunities to spend time in worship before, during and after involvement in conciliation processes will strengthen the spiritual connections of the team. Meetings for worship are central – and not an 'add-on' – to this work, which is an expression of Quaker faith in action.

The whole process of selecting and building a team involved in international conciliation takes time, commitment and belief in the process. Speaking about the component parts of the team with which he was working, Jan Arriens wrote:

> There was no hierarchy, even though Phil was a professional peaceworker, Diana had written books on the subject and was highly experienced, and Andrew had been General Secretary of Quaker Peace & Service for 17 years. We were all in this together. Talents and experience gravitated naturally towards where they could be used best. The issue we were dealing with came first.
>
> (Jan Arriens, paper prepared for
> the Woodbrooke consultation, 2019)

Skills and characteristics required in the team

A range of skills is required to undertake international conciliation, but they are not required of all members. An underlying set of skills is fundamental to participation in this kind of work. These skills include listening, the ability to maintain confidentiality, an attitude of understanding, and belief in the process.

Listening

Team members must have the capacity to listen to all sides, to 'hear' what is being said and to interpret any underlying messages. This requires team members to check with those with whom they are working and other team members to ensure that there is common understanding about what they are hearing.

> When Edith Wigzell was Quaker representative in Belfast, she and my wife Diana went to see a politician who had recently joined in a violent protest. He asked why they had come, and they explained that his actions had puzzled many people and they wanted to understand. He gave them the expected political rhetoric about his party's grievances, and added quickly, "Of course we each have our personal reasons too, but you wouldn't be interested in that." They said they would like to hear them if he was willing to tell. He then told them how he had been present when his best friend was killed by one of the other side's bombs. Beneath his anger he was carrying a deep sense of loss. When poisonous feelings are expressed and received in a loving, nonjudgmental spirit, and not countered, contradicted, or blamed, there is a moment of healing. As every counselor knows, the words a hurting person most needs to hear are his or her own. Working with ex-paramilitaries [we] became sharply aware of the burden of guilt and regrets which can follow violent actions. We found that an important part of our task was to be alongside them as they faced alcoholism and depression, remorse for deeds done, and qualms at betraying former loyalties.
>
> (Lampen, 2011: p. 22)

prayer

empathy

listening

hope

"When poisonous feelings are expressed and received in a loving, nonjudgmental spirit, and not countered, contradicted, or blamed, there is a moment of healing. As every counselor knows, the words a hurting person most needs to hear are his or her own."

Understanding nuances of language and having cultural awareness are part of this skill of listening. There is also the need for team members to find a common language within the group with whom they are working – with or without the assistance of interpreters. In one situation involving countries of the former Soviet Union, there was little communication between the leaders of the groups because they appeared to lack a common language. Eventually, the conciliators were able to build confidence within the group and everyone admitted that while they clung to their own languages, they could all in fact speak Russian. They had been reluctant to admit this because of their desire to identify with their cultural and linguistic differences. Once they acknowledged their shared understanding of Russian (the former oppressive power), the process could move forward.

Sue Williams, writing about her experiences in one situation, highlighted the need for a range of linguistic skills:

> Languages were important in several teams I worked in, though balance was important too: if one team member spoke Russian, for example, it was important that another spoke Georgian. It is difficult for intense people to convey their nuanced thoughts in a language which is not their own.
>
> (Sue Williams, paper prepared for
> the Woodbrooke consultation, 2019)

Stuart Morton recalled his own experiences with the hazards of using or not using interpreters. He referred to the need to check whether a translator would be needed:

> As I was the only one in the group who had previously visited the area and had long connections with some of the people, I was asked to make the introductory speech. The

person organising the meeting said that translation would not be needed; people would understand us. I spoke for a short time; I ensured my delivery was slow and as clear as I could make it. The meeting carried on with questions to us and responses by us. There was no obvious puzzlement on the faces of the audience – of about 70. After returning to London, perhaps two weeks later, I telephoned the person organising the meeting, but the phone was lifted by one of his senior colleagues. He asked me if I was the person who had first spoken to the group at the recent meeting. I affirmed that I was that person. He said, in clear English, something like, "We were discussing the day after the meeting what you had said, many of us could not understand you."

(Stuart Morton, paper prepared for
the Woodbrooke consultation, 2019)

A final point relating to listening concerns recording what has been heard. Not only do the members of the team have to 'hear' what is being said but they must also then accurately record from memory the content of the meetings, using language, writing and interpretation skills.

Confidentiality

Confidentiality raises many issues for individuals and teams. Material is confidential within the team, and how and when it is shared is often a dilemma that raises issues regarding truthfulness and honesty.

Understanding

It is essential to be able to walk alongside others in the conflict, being non-judgemental while remaining aware of their needs, and staying detached and objective throughout the process. Equally important are the skill of patience and the willingness to work at the speed of others, however frustrating this may be. Additionally, team members must also be able to recognise when there is a need to be flexible and change direction. Finally, the ability to stand back and recognise the lessons that have come from mistakes and lost opportunities is invaluable in this kind of work.

Belief in the process

International conciliation teams consist of members who have asked themselves various questions: Why do they want to do this type of work? What will they bring to it and what will they get from the experience? These are not casual questions but go to the root of the individual and their ability to contribute. There have been many examples of when these questions have not been asked by individuals and/or organisations, with serious consequences for the process.

In addition, team members must have a deep-rooted understanding of Quaker principles, experience of working in a team and well-rounded life experience. Ultimately, they must have a belief in the process and a willingness to work patiently with those seeking a nonviolent solution to the situation.

Ways of working

Beginning

Any involvement in international conciliation does not occur suddenly. It comes at the invitation of one or both parties involved in the conflict, who will have had prior contact with Quakers and

nonviolence

hope

courage

Team members must have a deep-rooted understanding
of Quaker principles… Ultimately, they must have a belief
in the process and a willingness to work patiently with
those seeking a nonviolent solution to the situation.

trust them sufficiently to believe that they will be able to help move the situation forward. With these existing relationships as a starting point, it is important to build contacts with decision-shapers from all sides. This is the case not only on the national level but also within local communities; it is a process of confidence building – listening, questioning and being ready to respond to any openings that emerge. All of those with something to contribute should be drawn into the process, including members of the diaspora and local peace groups. Meeting in safe places is of paramount importance, especially for those risking their lives by taking part in the process.

As with all such work, there is a need for careful analysis, setting clear and achievable objectives, developing time boundaries if possible, building in methods of evaluation, realistic planning, and ensuring that the work is held 'in the light'.

Process

Involvement in international conciliation is built on relationships and trust. Additionally, there is a need for honesty and confidentiality, but it cannot be assumed that this will apply to all participants at all times. However, it is essential that relationships and trust form the basis of Quaker participation; this is about letting everyone know with whom we are in contact, being open about who will be at meetings, and never saying one thing in one place and something else in another. Finding our role is part of the process. This may mean identifying the skills needed by those participating in the process and offering practical help, such as linking participating groups with literature or training to help them play their role. We must also recognise that within the violence of the conflict the images of the 'other' side are often distorted, and these perceptions may get in the way of progress. This needs to be addressed, and it may be a part of the conciliators' role to listen, interpret and explain.

Parties in conflict also are, in private, intrigued by the other parties, especially if they have no direct contact: what motivates them? Why do they take the positions they do? They desire to have an insight into them and their thinking. Mediators can help to bridge that gap. Discussions can be used to understand the other side, without revealing confidential conversations. By their questioning mediators can guide their interlocutors to think about the significant issues that face the other parties and to question why they behave as they do.

(Clem McCartney, paper prepared for
the Woodbrooke consultation, 2019)

Conciliators will generally need to attend meetings in neutral locations that are perceived as safe by those involved. Initially these will be with one 'side' at a time, so considerable travel will be involved – and often not by the most convenient route. For example, during the Nigerian Civil War, the Quaker conciliation team travelled to and from their meetings either directly from London to Lagos (when meeting with government representatives) or via Lisbon to another part of the same country (when having meetings with Biafran representatives), rather than travelling between the two venues within the country. This was partly for safety but also, more importantly, in order to demonstrate their neutrality.

Access to the country may be restricted because of difficulties with obtaining a visa or blocked by unexplained issues. Alternative venues acceptable and accessible to everyone may need to be identified. Agreeing a neutral location may be a positive development as it will not belong to any one side, weapons cannot be brought to the meeting and external issues are less likely to distract the participants.

Each situation brings its own issues, which have to be addressed and overcome. Maintaining contact with all levels in the process at all times is essential, and progress cannot be made if one side is reluctant to participate or has limited interest with no real desire to achieve a nonviolent solution. This may be difficult to recognise in the early stages of the process, but it may raise real issues about the viability of the process continuing once it becomes apparent.

Teams need to find the right balance between being intuitive and being analytical. Members must be ready to follow 'leadings' as they emerge, including unexpected leadings of the Spirit, but at the same time those leadings should be informed by a clear analysis of the situation and an understanding of the implications of different approaches.

Finding constructive ways to be critical is also important. One way to help that process is to be asked questions in a way that encourages us to test what we think we know and believe. This can shed a light on the limitations of our understanding.

Nurturing connections

Relationships not only have to be developed but also nurtured. The situation itself will constantly be changing and so will perceptions, understanding and interpretations of what is happening. Keeping in the loop, reading media reports, and maintaining links with those inside and outside the process who have specialist knowledge are the only ways to maintain knowledge of the situation and its players. This requires a time commitment that not everyone can afford, yet without this shared knowledge the team will not be able to function. Nurturing connections may also include repeated visits, checks of where everybody 'is' with their thinking and the impact of any new developments on the process. Regular visits will enable the nurturing of relationships on which the work is based.

Relationships do not remain static. They have to be nurtured, and assumptions should be handled with care.

Failure

This kind of work is long term and at times it will not be possible to see whether progress is being made. Additionally, not all efforts will come to a successful conclusion. It is important for the team to recognise when a particular relationship will never bear fruit, when a government will never allow an issue to progress or when the team is being used for other purposes. Sometimes there will be temporary lulls in the process. Whatever the reason, there is a need for ongoing, realistic reviews of the work to check that it is still viable. This may be painful for those who have committed an enormous amount of personal time and energy to the process. All conciliation work may reach a point where it has to be recognised that to continue will achieve nothing and may in fact be counter-productive. However, as Sue and Steve Williams wrote:

> Adam Curle describes one situation, the civil war in Nigeria-Biafra, where mediation appeared to have failed entirely, and one army was victorious. In retrospect, it appears that the mediation initiative may have helped to make possible a healing peace, by changing the perceptions of the Nigerian Army's leaders. This army, in turn, behaved in a most unexpected fashion:
>
> "Twice we thought we had a truce arranged; twice events on the battlefield aborted it. The war eventually ended militarily amid despairing fears of a massacre. But all predictions were wrong. Even now, I cannot speak without emotion of the way in which, instead of slaughtering the defeated Biafrans, the Federal Nigerian soldiers gave them food and money, cared

for them, took them to hospitals, treated them as brothers in the most wonderful spirit of reconciliation. Quakers were told by several people, whose judgement was reliable, that Quaker work over nearly three years of educating the two sides about each other and de-demonising both had filtered down from the leaders to the troops and contributed significantly to this miraculous outcome."

(Williams and Williams, 1994: p. 83)

Ending

Having taken the decision to end its involvement – whether it is because the process has come to a successful conclusion or, as mentioned above, because there seems to be no ongoing purpose to the involvement – the team must handle the ending as carefully as the beginning, and the timing is just as crucial.

Everyone must be informed of the team's withdrawal and shown that, if appropriate, the team would be willing to re-engage with the process. The relationships that have been tended carefully over a length of time need to be acknowledged and brought to a satisfactory ending.

All team members involved in the process will need to stand back and reflect on it. Learning should be gathered, and the stages of the process should be analysed and conclusions drawn from the piece of work. Endings can be painful, and, because of the confidential nature of the work, much cannot be shared beyond the small circle directly involved. However, the value of the time and energy invested should be recognised and acknowledged in some way.

Sometimes an ending is forced on a team when one of the groups with which it was working withdraws from the process. This may occur suddenly, without any explanation, as happened in one process of international conciliation with which Quakers were involved, which to that point seemed to have been progressing well. It was many years later that one of the members of the team was told in confidence by a local participant that there had been a rumour that Quakers were spies and had branches in many parts of the world. The trust had been broken and it was impossible to repair.

Another situation with which Quakers were involved was the conflict in what was then Southern Rhodesia (now Zimbabwe) in the 1970s. The conciliation process achieved its objectives; however, on reflection, those engaged in it felt that Quaker involvement had ended too soon. British Quakers felt a special responsibility for the citizens of the country, due to Britain's status as the colonial power in the country. British Friends had helped to establish Hlekweni, a rural training centre outside Bulawayo; local Friends were helping the families of political detainees; and Friends in Britain had met with exiled nationalists. In addition, Quakers had well-established connections with many within the country and the surrounding region.

A small group of Quakers worked, intensively at times, during the phases of the conciliation process. In 1976 there was a conference in Geneva convened by the British government to seek a way forward. All the main players were in attendance and the small team worked from QUNO Geneva over a ten-week period, building relationships, clarifying policies and facilitating communication between the parties.

No settlement was achieved, and the conciliation process moved back to Africa. There the team continued its work with all those involved in the process. They had access to key people and doors opened, which re-enforced their belief in the process. Additionally, building up and sustaining a wide range of contacts helped them to form a comprehensive picture of what was going on and enabled them to ask informed questions and make relevant comments. They remained with the process during the following years, making frequent visits to the region.

The situation evolved and in 1979 there was the possibility of a settlement and genuine independence elections. A conference was held between September and December at Lancaster House in London. Office facilities and support for the team were provided in the Africa Section at Friends House and a period of intensive activity commenced. During the conference, the team organised over 100 meetings with participants in support of the process:

> These [meetings] were with members of the British government, Foreign Office and Parliament, leading representatives of the Patriotic Front and the Muzorewa government, ambassadors or other representatives of front-line and other Commonwealth countries. In addition to this, letters were written, and telephone calls made. At last there was real hope of a breakthrough and our role had become that of a lubricant – by identifying sticking points and where appropriate, making representation with a view to problems being overcome rather than used as a reason to break off negotiations. There were, in fact, two or three occasions when a breakdown seemed possible, especially over the ceasefire arrangements, but in the event, agreement was reached.
>
> (Trevor Jepson, 'Quaker experience of political mediation', confidential document, 1989)

"You Quakers kept alive in our minds the idea that a negotiated settlement was possible at the darkest time, when there was only war."

Two comments were subsequently reported to Quaker Peace & Service:

> One of the African leaders said afterwards, "You Quakers kept alive in our minds the idea that a negotiated settlement was possible at the darkest time, when there was only war."

> Adam Curle was once told by someone from the diplomatic community who did not know that he was a Quaker, that the Quakers had played a significant part in helping the process which led to a settlement.
>
> (Trevor Jepson, 'Quaker experience of political mediation', confidential document, 1989)

Zimbabwe faced considerable challenges in rebuilding its society after many years of conflict and the process of reconciliation. Friends opened a Quaker Friendship Centre in Harare to support reconciliation. After a couple of years, this work was discontinued. However, as mentioned above, those involved with the Quaker conciliation team then, and others since, have reflected on the process and felt that Quakers' withdrawal was too quick. More might have been done to address the violence and disruption by using existing relationships and skills to explore alternatives. Some have felt that an opportunity was lost.

Risk

The very nature of this work involves risks for those involved. The decision-making process in response to any request for Quakers to become involved with a new international conciliation process must include a risk assessment relating to the process, the individuals who might make up the team, and the organisation. It is important that those involved do not take avoidable risks or put others in danger.

The parties with whom conciliators work are very aware of the risks they run just by becoming involved in the process. They may even risk their own lives if others involved, including members of their own group, feel that they are reaching out too far to the other side. They are very aware of these risks and take them into account at all stages in the process.

Quakers who are involved in conciliation processes also, at times, put themselves at personal risk. They have to be aware of the level of risk and decide how willing they are to put themselves in challenging situations. This applies to individuals but is also a team decision. Those line-managing the process may have to step in to intervene when the team is prepared to take greater risks than the organisation is comfortable with supporting. The organisation has a duty of care to those carrying out work on its behalf, and there is also the possibility of reputational risk for the organisation itself – all of this has to be taken into consideration.

In her paper for the Woodbrooke consultation, Sue Williams wrote:

> Over time, I/we had to come to grips with a feeling that we were exposing our local colleagues to danger. In reality, we were all in danger just by being there. They reminded us that, like us, they were intelligent adults, and able to decide how much risk to take, and it was, after all, their country. We were lucky to have such collegial and equal relationships. Still, when colleagues were harmed or killed, we always went through it again. In Northern Ireland, we had to recognise the luxury of not feeling worried, when interlocutors from both sides were keenly aware of being in danger. This field of work presents many dilemmas.
>
> (Sue Williams, paper prepared for the Woodbrooke consultation, 2019)

Dilemmas

At many stages of the process, those involved (the individual, the team or the organisation) will face dilemmas. These dilemmas may be thrown up by the situation, by those with whom the conciliators are working or by personal responses to challenging circumstances. Some can be anticipated in advance, but the strength of the team and the supporting organisation enable other dilemmas to be addressed as they emerge.

Undertaking this type of work sometimes raises the moral dilemma of appearing to collude with evil. Developing relationships with individuals or groups who have committed atrocities in order to forward the conciliation process may seem to make them and their actions legitimate. This is challenging for the team and in some circumstances may form a reputational risk for Quakers and their other work.

Carrying messages may also threaten to compromise the team. For example, how are team members being used? Are their attempts to reach a nonviolent solution being undermined by the agendas of others? These are dilemmas that need to be discussed ahead of the process so that the team has the strength of thought-through responses.

> How do we recognise the best times to take initiatives? Is it ever acceptable to act as couriers for secret documents? How do we know if we are being 'used'? Assuming that there are extremists and moderates on both sides, should our limited resources be used primarily to strengthen the moderates or 'unharden the hearts of the extremists'? Should we encourage moderates to take risks to promote

peace, which could expose them to great personal risks from extremists? Initiatives are confidential. Other Friends will recognise the need for advocacy or human rights work which, when undertaken in the name of Quakers will appear to be inappropriate if not hostile. Can we make a choice between human rights and conciliation and stick firmly to one rather than trying to do both? Could others undertake the human rights work? There might be a legitimate expectation of local Friends to be involved (or to abstain from involvement) and whether or not this is appropriate.

('Quaker experience of political mediation', confidential document, 1989)

The team members will be aware of the risks that might be taken by some of the participants (see above) and at times this will create dilemmas for the team. Should they help individuals to flee from a dangerous situation? How far should they place others at risk by engaging them in the process? If the team learns of a planned attack, what should it do with this information? Alongside these and similar possibilities is the dilemma of determining whether an intervention at a particular point would help or make the situation worse.

Confidentiality underpins any international conciliation process, but the work may not be undertaken in isolation. Local Friends may be aware of or be involved in the process. However, time will be needed to build relationships with local Friends in order to ensure that they have the information needed to support the process without compromising confidentiality.

As mentioned in chapter 2, one underlying principle of conciliation is that conciliators should be impartial. However, while attempting to remain impartial, this creates dilemmas for those working in situations where there are or have been atrocities and human rights abuses. Conciliators approach the situation from a position of principled impartiality, and those with whom they are working should be helped to understand this. This challenge for Quakers involved in international conciliation leads to a dilemma about purity, as addressed by Sue Williams in her paper for the consultation:

> The purity dilemma: Quakers, like most people, fill different roles in different situations, which present different dilemmas. When we are taking symbolic actions, it may be vital to be completely transparent. One of our ideals is the famous phrase: speak truth to power. However, mediation is much more pragmatic than symbolic, and depends more on listening than lecturing. The first dilemma of purity in a mediation context is that, while we might say it is always best to be transparent, for mediators it may be necessary to settle for being honest. The second dilemma is that we are representing a group which has established a reputation over centuries. Is our main aim to preserve that reputation, or to put it to work in the world of mediation to try to build peace? Our view, my view, is that the reputation makes it possible for us to be trusted, and that it therefore obliges us to do something with it. Unfortunately, some Quakers don't want their representatives to meet with 'bad guys'. Why can't you work with nonviolent people, they ask? Well, we do, but if we really want to promote peace, we need to engage with the violent people, also. Fortunately, different Quakers can be doing different things, even in the same context. When peace processes have some success, it is usually because lots of different people try lots of different things, sometimes seeming to be working in opposite directions. It is difficult, because as representatives we are taking advantage of the

reputation of Quakers, hoping to strengthen it, but not always sure of this. (I will add that this dilemma has its consequences on a personal level as well. I feel acutely the loss of the ideal of purity, even as I acknowledge the necessity of it when mediating in a war, and appreciate that, for me, the loss has been worth it.)

(Sue Williams, paper prepared for
the Woodbrooke consultation, 2019)

Quakers may come under pressure to take a public position in relation to a particular situation. Their traditional role of sitting in the background, enabling and facilitating, does not sit easily with such a public role. At times, this can present a real dilemma for a team engaged in conciliation.

Another dilemma is the need to commit to a piece of work that may or may not be completed or reach a conclusion:

An overarching dilemma is that this kind of initiative rarely succeeds, and never quickly. We were fortunate enough that our twenty years in Northern Ireland began with parties who had never spoken to each other and moved from violence to ceasefires to a peace agreement. The society itself changed over this time, to begin addressing some of the most important grievances and injustices. And it was the collective, synergistic impact of all sorts of people that produced results. People in other situations work just as hard, just as well, and they may not see improvement. We ourselves added our work in many countries, and some got better, and some did not.

(Sue Williams, paper prepared for
the Woodbrooke consultation, 2019)

A dilemma faced by both individual and organisational Quaker peacemakers is the possible conflict between whether they should be prophets or reconcilers. Both roles have their part to play and Quakers can move between the two. However, a Quaker cannot be in both roles at the same time. For more on this, see Grigor McClelland's paper from Yearly Meeting 1960, 'Our historic witness in 1660–1960', and Wolf Mendl's 1974 Swarthmore Lecture, *Prophets and reconcilers: Reflections on the Quaker peace testimony.*

Sometimes, the issues at the root of the conflict lead Quakers to feel that they should campaign about the injustice and violence facing them. Trying to balance the two approaches can be challenging for the individual, and the choice as to which role to adopt has been highlighted in a paper produced for the author by Diana Francis:

> My personal view is that in a given situation we need to ask ourselves what we can contribute most usefully in relation to the conflict in question. If a particular opportunity comes along, for an individual or organisation, to contribute in a potentially important way to positive change – even a breakthrough – in a particular role and context, then although that may be in an unexpected or counter-intuitive way, one should think carefully before turning it down.

> I spent my earlier life in campaigning and nonviolent activism, and the triumph of nonviolence in the second half of the 1980s and early 1990s, in the ousting of President Marcos in the Philippines and in the gradual dissolution of the former Soviet empire, more than confirmed the much earlier demonstrations of its power under the leadership of Mahatma Gandhi and Martin Luther King. When, however, the lives of ordinary people did not improve in those regions and new

and dangerous conflicts emerged, I, along with many others, realised that new, destructive conflicts were emerging which, though often taken advantage of by ambitious demagogues, were mutually destructive and needed a very different approach.

We therefore saw the need to broaden the focus of our nonviolent responses and recognise that not only is dialogue an essential tool of nonviolence in overcoming injustice – in building alliances and engaging with those in power – but that we needed to develop the skills of facilitation and mediation, both to enable people to work together and to bring conflicting sides together when that is in the interest of both. The skills of advocacy, civil courage and persuasion can also be harnessed in these apparently very different ways.

In the case of the new nationalist divisions that began to emerge in the former Yugoslavia, those who, in 1991, formed the Center for Anti-War Action in Belgrade, not only campaigned against the warmongering and aggression of Slobodan Milošević but set up a section called MOST or 'bridge', which worked through the war to support refugees from other parts of the region and resist the alienation between different identity groups that was being fomented by their governments. I was asked to go as a trainer to help them learn to do that but found they needed very little – just some new ways of analysing things and channelling the skills they already had.

Being in the middle may seem to require less courage and assertiveness than being a campaigner but that is not always so. In face-to-face meetings, a mediator or facilitator has the job of 'holding the ring' in which the different parties can safely encounter each other. That may at times involve challenging unhelpful or aggressive behaviour. Equally, campaigners need to be able to communicate winningly as well as challenge and defuse anger in those they encounter (for instance, the police).

There can of course be dilemmas about what role to take. The two criteria for me are whether I believe that the impact of what I am doing is beneficial and whether I can in practice manage my own personal feelings in a particular context to play the role that is required of me.

For decades I have been a passionate advocate of respect for different sexual identities and orientations, my feelings on the subject only intensified by the fact that one of my daughters is a lesbian. I witnessed at close hand all the difficulties she faced at school and beyond and the courage it took for her to grow into the delightful, grounded, passionate and kind person she has become.

I had facilitated two international trainings for the World Council of Churches (WCC) at its centre at Bossey, near Geneva. Then one day I received a request to facilitate an international dialogue for the WCC on human sexuality, in the wake of the explosion of angry contention at its International Assembly in Harare, Zimbabwe, where homosexuality was outlawed. A commission had been set up to explore the issue and this dialogue was set up as part of that exploration. In the event it brought together clergy and lay members not only from a range of Protestant churches but also two or three Orthodox priests and one senior cleric from a Catholic seminary.

I was in no doubt as to the importance of the dialogue, but my natural inclination would have been to be an advocate for one side of the argument. However, they had plenty of those. I was being asked instead to play an enabling role for those coming from deeply held and opposing positions. The question I had to ask myself was whether I would be able to step aside from my own viewpoint and feelings in order to do what was asked of me.

I decided I could and was so glad that I had. The dialogue process, which we structured with care and which lasted for several days, was tense to begin with, and included some strongly articulated conservative 'official' positions; but through the courage of the personal testimony of individuals and the atmosphere of quiet listening that had been established between us, the sessions became increasingly open and honest and there was a powerful recognition of the humanity of all present. We had become one community of learning.

I particularly remember that the Catholic priest said his mind had been completely changed and that what he told his students from then on would be quite different from what he had taught them before. I believe that that dialogue process changed far more than a campaign could have done and felt privileged to have been involved.

(Diana Francis, unpublished paper, 2019)

Organisational responsibilities

The focus of this chapter so far has been on the work and the conciliators themselves, but both exist within a context and form part of an organisation's programme. The organisation itself has responsibilities, and any engagement with new opportunities for international conciliation should not be undertaken lightly. Once a request for assistance has been received, it has to be set against the organisation's existing priorities, and challenging questions need to be addressed, including:

- How would the work fit in with other existing or planned projects?
- Does the organisation have the expertise and professionalism to support such work?
- Are people with the relevant skills available to undertake it?

Any such decisions should not be made in isolation but within the structure of the yearly meeting, with committees overseeing the work and with networks of local Friends meetings.

In the past it was possible to embark on international conciliation programmes without major constraints of time or finance. However, more recently, organisational demands have come to require that any new piece of work has clearly expressed priorities and objectives including budgets and outlines of other costs. The relevant committee and staff need to explore the request before making a firm commitment. The purpose is to check the work's viability, whether the conciliators have a role to play and whether it is work that could be undertaken by Friends. Ultimately it is part of the role of the organisation to ensure that, before proceeding, plans for the work, budgets, regular evaluation, and plans for how the project will be closed have been considered in detail.

Once the work is underway, the role of the organisation shifts to that of support and oversight. The international conciliators need to feel that they have a secure base that will provide them with the structure needed to underpin their work. This structure comes from the appointment of a small committee of Quakers as a reference group (with an awareness of the political, social and economic setting and able to provide spiritual support for those engaged in the process) and a line manager with experience of international conciliation. While acknowledging that there is a need for short- and long-term targets, it is important that the organisation recognises that this type of work is slow and time consuming, so as to avoid unrealistic expectations. There are opportunities but also limitations in this type of work.

In order to enable the work – which has financial costs – to continue, there is a need for the programme to be financially stable. There has to be an organisational commitment to the work, and it should not be subject to any sudden or unexpected financial cuts. Therefore, a funding plan should be put in place at the outset.

There may, at times, be conflict within the organisation – for example, when the need to maintain confidentiality comes up against the need-to-know sharing of information with others not directly involved with the work. There may also be a dilemma with advocacy work in the same region cutting across the conciliation work. Such conflicts must be resolved by the organisation.

Alongside these structural and financial underpinnings, the organisation should provide supervision and the personal and spiritual support needed by those engaged in the work. The efforts may be a considerable drain, both physically and emotionally, on those involved in the process, and this should be recognised. Organisations should provide opportunities to discuss dilemmas and, if required, professional assistance with the psychological impact of the work.

"...there was a powerful recognition of the humanity of all present."

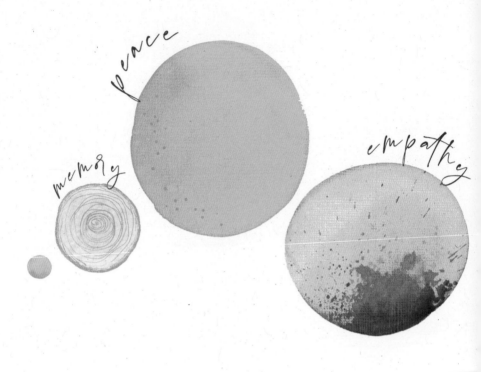

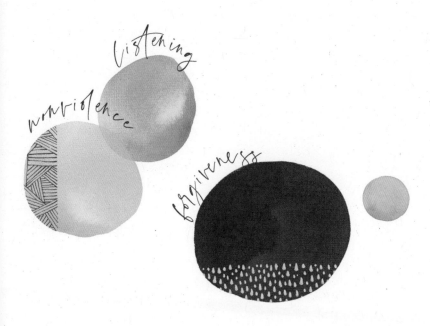

listening

nonviolence

forgiveness

Evaluation

As indicated above, international conciliation should include evaluation as part of the process from its inception. However, like other types of Quaker work, it is extremely difficult to evaluate. It is tricky to use a scientific form of evaluation (often used in other international programmes) when evaluating a faith-based approach. Tools used in other evaluation processes may not be easily transferable. However, the fact that the available tools are not always useful does not mean that international conciliation should not be reviewed and evaluated. How else will those involved with the organisation and Quaker donors know if it is continuing to be viable? Or whether the work should continue or be laid down?

There are many different tools available to adapt for the purposes of evaluating Quaker conciliation work. This section outlines just two of them.

Diana Francis used the following questions to underpin a review of such projects:

- How deeply Quaker is this work?
- Is it grounded in the life of the Spirit?
- Does it uphold Quaker testimonies?

She used the answers to these questions as the basis of her evidence in her report to QPSW Central Committee.

Another tool – set out in the book *Working with conflict* (Fisher et al., 2000) – provides a framework that helps to conceptualise the process of evaluation in a series of questions:

- What is the vision of the project?
- What are the values that guide and inform the vision?
- Are the vision and values known to/shared by all stakeholders?
- Do the goals reflect the vision and values?
- What are the activities undertaken?
- At which levels are the activities undertaken?
- Are the values and vision reflected in activities at all levels?
- Are the activities helping to achieve the goals?
- What are the indicators to assess progress towards goals?
- Are the goals and indicators known to/shared by the actors at all levels?
- Who has set the indicators, and at which levels?
- Are the resources (human/material) appropriate/adequate for the activities?
- What is the focus of change and is it taking place? If not, what needs to happen now?

(Fisher et al., 2000: pp. 161–162)

Setting aims and objectives along with indicators at the beginning of the process will strengthen the organisation's oversight.

Modern tools of evaluation – and even the concept that they should be in place – would not have formed part of the thinking of those involved with international conciliation in the past. However, much has changed. Nowadays, along with a need to control budgets, determine priorities and use scarce resources well, organisations have to have mechanisms to ensure that their work continues to fulfil their overall purpose. Therefore, although difficult to evaluate, it is essential that any international conciliation process has within its structure the capacity to provide evidence relevant to any discussions about its validity.

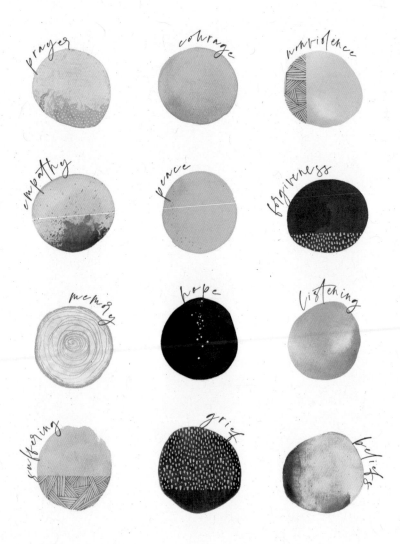

Chapter 4

Opportunities for future work in a changing world

Brian Phillips set out his vision for the five defining qualities of Quaker global witness in the 21st century:

- identifying those who can make a change
- a ministry of presence
- continuity of commitment
- acts of faith, and
- pragmatic approaches to reconciliation (Phillips, 2006: pp. 9–24).

Brian Phillips' list of defining qualities encompasses Quakers' traditional roles as prophets and reconcilers. Quakers have a long history of achievements, and the challenge for today is how to apply these roles in the 21st century. How does Quaker international conciliation fit in with this vision?

As one of the historic Peace Churches, Quakers have in the past engaged with others to address major issues of the day, such as slavery and prison reform. Friends' commitment to peace and nonviolent processes to achieve Spirit-led 'leadings' has enabled them to engage with decision-makers and decision-shapers nationally and internationally in spite of being numerically small. Quakers have been ready to walk alongside others who do not share their views, engaging and listening while not compromising their own position.

Many of the issues addressed in the past were unpopular – ahead of their time – but were expressions of Quakers' faith in action. The same is true today. British Quakers' commitment to same-sex relationships and marriage is an expression of the testimony to equality; however, for some other Churches and Quakers in other parts of the world, it is a step too far. Nevertheless, just as Quakers in the past committed to quiet, long-term processes – combining their roles as prophets and reconcilers – in order to enact change, the same is being done today. The principles remain the same: it is ongoing revelation that inspires and informs.

Over the centuries, Quakers' reputation has opened doors, and Friends' input has been respected, even if not always accepted. This consistency of faith-based action has been acknowledged; Quakers have built up 'credit' (as mentioned in chapter 1). They have used this credit to access and contribute to discussions about issues of concern both nationally and internationally. However, like all credit, it is a finite resource and should be used wisely to achieve Spirit-led goals. How will Quakers use their remaining credit in the 21st century? The present continues to produce challenges. However, with a declining membership and shifting priorities, what future work will Quakers feel 'called' to do?

The world's political structures are in a process of change. In recent years, numerous phenomena have all contributed to this change and prompted options for future intervention. Examples include the fracturing of power blocs, globalisation and anti-globalisation, the rise of radical movements without any visible leaders or borders, increasing economic disparities, the climate crisis, the power of international corporations, and the impact of social media in informing action at local, national and international levels.

In this rapidly changing world, Quakers need to stand back and reflect before determining the way forward in their national and international work. Is what Friends are offering still relevant? It could be argued that at a time of unrest and uncertainty, there is a greater need for those involved in violent conflict to have the opportunity to meet in a neutral space with skilled conciliators. Conciliation is one tool that Quakers might offer. However, it is not their only tool. There are many others available. As Andrew Tomlinson, director of Quaker United Nations Office (QUNO) New

Just as Quakers in the past committed to quiet, long-term processes in order to enact change, the same is being done today. The principles remain the same: it is ongoing revelation that inspires and informs.

York, said at the Woodbrooke consultation, "conciliation is part of an orchestra working for social change".

The world itself is changing, with a reduction of opportunities for traditional forms of international conciliation. Additionally, there are other institutions and organisations (both faith-based and secular) that are involved with research, analysis of conflicts and international conciliation; these groups have all also built up bodies of knowledge and skills. This area of work has become professionalised. Is there still a space for Quakers to continue in this work?

Quakers are a small organisation, but they have considerable experience and a desire to continue with this work. It is important that Quakers should not be so committed to what they have done in the past that they fail to see opportunities to use their accumulated skills and knowledge in the future. Earlier attempts to rebuild the Diplomats Programme in London did not thrive because the world had changed. Quakers should not only look to the past for connections but also to existing areas of work. Where are the connections today that might provide opportunities to build the relationships of trust that will be needed in the future?

At the Woodbrooke consultation, QUNO gave examples of how its staff had addressed huge problems facing the world, such as land mines and climate change – issues that were already oversubscribed in terms of the number of organisations working on them. In order to avoid repeating what others were doing, it was important for QUNO to look for a new or different focus to take the work forward. Similarly, international conciliation should build on existing connections and remain open to using them creatively.

Friends have, as a starting point, the relationships developed at the international institutions where there are Quaker offices, at the United Nations and the European Union. Within their own networks, Quakers have developed close connections through their work in relation to social justice, sustainability, economic justice, climate change, ecumenical accompaniment, support for nonviolent action in Britain and East Africa, refugees and migrants, an understanding of the origins of violence, and support for peace education and peer mediation. Quakers have a wide range of connections that might provide opportunities for international conciliation work in the future. The danger for a small organisation with many demands on its resources is that unless there is a vision of what might be possible as a result of international conciliation work, other criteria might be used to refocus the organisation's resources. As a result, opportunities may be lost or fail to thrive because energy and resources have been diverted elsewhere.

If Quakers are approached to assist in a situation, the next question is: are the necessary human and organisational resources available to take it forward? Is there a pool of Quakers with the skills, experience, professionalism, commitment, and availability to contribute to this work? Such people exist but need to be nurtured and supported.

One of the concerns that arose during the Woodbrooke consultation was how to recruit and prepare the next generation of Quakers to be involved in international conciliation. Some people are already involved with international conciliation within faith-based or secular organisations, and one of the participants commented that his work was "very similar to what Quakers are doing. The unique and important thing about Quaker conciliation is that it's done by Quakers. [We should] celebrate the fact that there are places where we can do the work" (participant comment, Woodbrooke consultation, 2019). He and others in a similar situation suggested that they might be brought in when a specific piece of Quaker work is under consideration. Primarily, their need was for support in their work as Quakers involved with non-Quaker international conciliation. This was discussed at the consultation and possible ways of providing this support were considered and will be taken forward.

There are a number of existing programmes that might provide an entry point for younger Quakers who would like to become involved in international conciliation. For example, in one programme, peaceworkers are placed with peace organisations in Britain for one year to gain experience. By the end of their placement, they have acquired many of the skills required. Similarly, the programme assistants at QUNO and Quaker Council for European Affairs have a year's opportunity to develop a deeper understanding of the issues and ways of working in off-the-record meetings. There are many young Quakers with experience of peace work with a range of organisations, and others who have participated in Quaker activities.

These individuals' energy and desire to become part of a pool of future international conciliators has to be recognised by the organisation with some preparation, training and encouragement. This is time-consuming for both the individuals and the organisation but essential for the future of the work. It was suggested at the Woodbrooke consultation that it might be possible for some to be included in teams as non-travelling members. This might give them the opportunity to learn about the challenges, issues, approaches, and opportunities of international conciliation work. This suggestion was popular, and it was hoped that it could be taken forward. However, there are implications relating to the nominations process, people's availability for such volunteer activity, the level of commitment required at a time when those involved are developing their own careers, and the demands on existing conciliators and the organisation. Finally, the ability of the organisation to support the work should be considered. There is a need for staff and committees to provide oversight, and sufficient budgetary capacity is needed to underwrite the work.

The focus of this book has been on Quaker international conciliation and the challenges confronted in a changing world. Quakers continue to receive requests for assistance. However, growing levels of training and involvement of local people in conflicts within their own regions, and concerns about the impact of long-distance flights on the environment, have raised questions about whether Quakers should continue their involvement in this work in the future. Friends should consider each new request carefully, being aware that openings may come because Quakers are perceived to have the skills needed by those involved in the conflict even if the opportunity may not 'fit' the structures and budget of the organisation. Quaker work has always been Spirit-led.

Quakers continue to have the knowledge, skills and commitment to peace required to undertake conciliation work, and these skills might be used within a national context. Britain is experiencing a fracturing of its society, a threat to its national cohesion and growing intolerance of difference. As such, there may be opportunities for a pool of people to use the experience gained over many years in an international setting. Quakers might offer quiet spaces, neutral settings, confidentiality, and a commitment to a process that takes as long as is needed. The same range of skills and processes as were set out in chapter 3 would be needed – only the setting would be different. In the past, Quaker centres or houses were used for these purposes and might be a way forward within Britain to complement work already being done by Quakers and others at a local level, as mentioned in the introduction.

Quakers in Britain are at a significant stage in their history. They have a vision of the world and their place in it, and of what they could contribute – building on their past and open to opportunities in the future. They have a commitment to peace and to 'that of God in everyone'. It is challenging to express this commitment in work and witness in national and international settings, but Quakers have much to offer. It is important that as they determine on what and where they should work, their rich heritage is not lost in the process. Opportunities for long-term international work should not be curtailed because of short-term decisions made in the present.

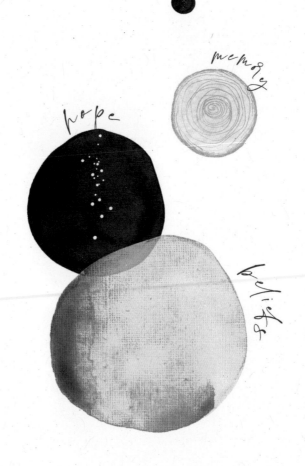

hope

memory

beliefs

Chapter 5

The Woodbrooke consultation

The consultation took place from 15 to 18 September 2019 at Woodbrooke Quaker Study Centre in Birmingham. Forty-two participants were brought together with the intention to:

- hold an "intergenerational exchange for Quaker peacemakers about international conciliation work"
- "pass on knowledge to younger people who have already demonstrated interest"
- "collect ideas relating to future Quaker conciliation", and
- "capture the learning in a publication aimed primarily at British Quakers" (Conference materials).

There had been a consultation 30 years earlier at Jordans Quaker Centre. This event was restricted to experienced practitioners of Quaker international conciliation, and as a result their knowledge and skills were shared with only a very small group of people.

The Woodbrooke consultation was larger and included a wider and more diverse group of people, and in the process shone a light on this important but largely unknown area of Quaker work. It brought together the reflections of Quakers currently working on international conciliation processes and the experiences of younger Quakers involved with various forms of peace work. It provided a space for those present to explore ways of applying the accumulated skills and knowledge in a rapidly changing world. The peaceful setting of Woodbrooke enhanced the experience of those participating in the conference, and everyone was fully engaged with the topic, the challenges and possible ways forward.

The consultation was a mixture of talks, presentations, international video and/or telephone links, and inspiring papers from participants unable to attend in person. There were also panel discussions, small group work and imaginative exercises looking at the past 30 years of

Quaker international work, exploring the possibility of future work, and examining the skills of a conciliator. Finally, there was time for challenging and thought-provoking conversations over meals and between sessions. During the conference, some individuals were interviewed for a short video to be produced by Britain Yearly Meeting, the purpose of which will be to raise awareness of Quaker international conciliation work and conciliation work in general, and to promote the book.

It would be impossible to re-tell the details of the conference in full as there is always the danger that in recounting the events it would seem, to the general reader, the equivalent of looking at other people's holiday photos – memorable for those who took them but not so interesting for the viewer. This chapter therefore aims to record the events in broad brush strokes, conveying the essence and some of the substance so that those who were there, and the general reader, are left with an impression of what transpired and the outcomes.

Sydney Bailey, one of the participants at the Jordans consultation in 1989, wrote:

> Until recent times, wars were usually fought for territory, occasionally for the dynastic interests of rulers. Now they are more often fought because of the perception that human rights are being denied.

> It is partly for this reason that many armed conflicts nowadays are not wars between states but internal conflicts between communities differing in ethnic origin, language, religion, or some other distinguishing feature – witness events in Sri Lanka, Lebanon, South Africa, Cyprus and Northern Ireland.
>
> (Bailey, 1989: p. 585)

Since 1989 we have seen an increase in the challenges of a changing world. We are facing the globalisation of conflicts, the increasing use of social media and the rise of movements dedicated to destruction.

Aküm Longchari, a participant at the Woodbrooke consultation, set out the context for groups living within a state where they are the minority. He outlined the perceptions of many indigenous and minority groups who feel that they originated as a caravan, which was taken over at some point in their history and made to change their course of travel. They have the dilemma of either trying to go back to the point at which they were hijacked or continuing on their present path. Another option is to create a new direction.

Aküm felt that people are traumatised by their experiences over the generations and that this makes it difficult for them to move from where they are to the negotiating table. He spoke at length about the way in which governments deal with minority groups, often attempting a range of tactics to separate potential leaders from the people they are trying to represent, with the aim of maintaining the status quo.

Aküm told the story of a time when he was in Vietnam and visited a village after a massacre. All of those with him wanted to help and asked what they could do. They were told by the village leaders to think of living under a large waterfall and offering to help with buckets. The village did not need buckets – it needed help with going to the source of the waterfall and finding out how to reduce its volume. Aküm linked this idea to Quaker involvement in conciliation.

He described his own positive experiences of working with Quaker conciliators, and his talk set the scene for many of the following discussions. The conference moved on to explore a couple of different ways in which conciliation can take place, in different settings but using similar skills.

Long-term conciliation processes

Jan Arriens, a former diplomat and a member of the Quaker Peace & Social Witness (QPSW) Conciliation Group since 2007, described the difference between his previous work and his work with QPSW:

> For all my familiarity with international dealings, I found myself in a different world. I thought it might be illuminating if I begin by looking at some of the fundamental differences between working as a diplomat and working as a Quaker peaceworker.

> In this unfamiliar world, I would, had it been left to me, have lined the armed factions up on opposite sides of the room, with civil society representatives in between. Each group would have been invited to express their grievances; we would have faced the key differences head on. Subject to certain ground rules, there might then have been some very sharp exchanges, even taking the conference to breaking point, combined with some shuttle diplomacy.

> Instead we began with an exercise involving the scoping of hopes, needs and fears. As a new boy on the group, and coming from an entirely different tradition, I kept my views to myself. I was however somewhat mystified and found that a number of the civil society people with whom we were working were also wondering what was going on. What were all these flipcharts about, and where were we going? It all seemed very slow.

I remember one occasion when Diana Francis and I had to facilitate a session on forgiveness. Potentially, this was a key session. How were we to approach it? Once again, I found myself confronted by techniques that were unfamiliar and uncomfortable. At one point I remember exploding and taking Diana to task about "footling Western models". Diana, ruefully but with great generosity, agreed that that was what they were. After almost reaching deadlock, we eventually hit on the formula of asking them to explain what form forgiveness took in their society. In other words, we would stand back and look at forgiveness in a kind of sociological and anthropological light.

I made some pompous little speech to introduce the session along those lines and then threw out that question. "What did forgiveness mean in their context?" The question was ignored – instead people spoke from the heart about their own experience. It was electrifying. There was great emotion in the room, and a deep sharing. Those moments, when we had gone out of our way to avoid confrontation and the airing of grievances, could, in retrospect, be said to have marked the beginnings of the reconciliation process. That was lesson one: listen to my colleagues; accept that preconceived ideas might not work.

(Jan Arriens, paper prepared for
the Woodbrooke consultation, 2019)

Jan continued by giving details of working in the team and his experiences of the Quakers' lengthy time frame, which he compared with how things worked when he was a diplomat:

A posting in Southeast Asia was for two years and elsewhere for three. There was no long-term continuity. I had four

forgiveness

People spoke from the heart about their
own experience. It was electrifying.

postings in all, and found that in each case it took me about six months to get fully into stride. Inevitably, there was a period of winding down towards the end, so that one's full effectiveness could be limited to little more than a year.

(Jan Arriens, paper prepared for
the Woodbrooke consultation, 2019)

Drawing extensively on his experiences as a Quaker conciliator, he outlined the nature of the work and its impact on those with whom he worked and on himself and his colleagues as conciliators:

Certain truths emerge: the unity of all things and our essential interconnectedness, the certainty that the higher level of consciousness by which we are embraced and of which we form part is benevolent, and the fact that the great unifying force and manifestation of the transcendent is love. Certain guiding principles for life emerge from these truths. These include a belief in equality, love, compassion, and a sacramental approach to life. These principles are also brought out most beautifully and powerfully in the life and teachings of Jesus. It is from this level of awareness that our testimonies are derived. In the end, though, it is the still small voice to which we testify through our actions.

(Jan Arriens, paper prepared for
the Woodbrooke consultation, 2019)

Jan concluded his talk with the following statement:

Our overseas work forms part of our shared spiritual experience as Quakers in Britain. It has been a living out of what we believe. It has taken us beyond the confines of our immediate, local concerns, and has shown how constancy and commitment can achieve things that guns and threats cannot. It is, to my mind, a matter for deep concern that our overseas work has shrunk as it has over the past 20 or so years. I feel the spiritual life of our dear Society has suffered as a result. I can see why this should have happened, and I can see that it will be extremely difficult to reverse the trend. But reverse it I feel we should, not just for the fullness of our spiritual expression, both individually and as a body of Friends, but also because humanity's response to the huge challenges facing the world must, in the end, have a spiritual foundation or all will be in vain. We must take our tradition forward, in the knowledge that the leadings of the Spirit are needed more than ever before. I profoundly hope that the need for, and the future of, overseas peace and conciliation work will be a matter for discernment by the full body of Friends in Britain Yearly Meeting. I hope and pray that this gathering will help show the way.

(Jan Arriens, paper prepared for
the Woodbrooke consultation, 2019)

The talk was followed by a number of plenary and small group sessions. These looked at the skills and knowledge Quaker conciliators had developed over the years, the ways in which similar work is carried out in secular and other faith organisations, the opportunities presented for Quakers working in non-Quaker settings, and the challenges faced by conciliators whatever the setting.

Small circles: Quaker conciliation work in international institutions

I pin my hopes to quiet processes and small circles, in which vital and transforming events take place.

quiet processes and small circles

"I pin my hopes to quiet processes and small circles,
in which vital and transforming events take place."

(Rufus Jones, extract from a letter written to Violet Holdsworth, 1937, quoted in *Quaker faith & practice* 24.56)

Staff from Quaker United Nations Office (QUNO) Geneva, QUNO New York and Quaker Council for European Affairs (QCEA) in Brussels led a session on their work. They are building on a long history of off-the-record meetings, which usually take place over a meal and provide a safe space for diplomats to explore issues. Their work is eased because "our reputation opens doors as our predecessors have made a huge footprint" (Florence Foster, Representative for Peace & Disarmament, QUNO Geneva).

The representatives outlined how they work:

- They work in teams, never alone, because they need a sounding board to reflect on the process, and this corporate discernment is a characteristic of Quaker work.
- They create a shared framework or culture for the team. They have shared values and a common understanding and trust of each other.
- The work is time consuming as it involves detailed preparation and sharing.

The teams work on a variety of issues, and the speakers drew from these to illustrate ways in which they approach each process. They do not take on every issue being discussed at the United Nations (UN) or European Union (EU) but apply criteria informally known as the Rachel Brett (former Representative for Human Rights at QUNO Geneva) principles, which are that Quakers should only do work if:

- it is unique because no one else is doing it, and
- they bring something others do not.

A number of examples were given during the conference of how these principles have been put into practice. Two are included here to illustrate aspects of their work: one more recent (an example of a one-off meeting) and the other a process that has been completed.

Olivia Caeymaex, Peace Programme Director of QCEA in Brussels, spoke of her work:

> In exploring the role of the EU in contentious regions around the world, QCEA organised an event on the path to peace for an occupied territory, at Quaker House, Brussels. The EU is one of the primary actors involved in trade, development and humanitarian assistance in that region. Our work took place in a context of not only different perspectives by local and third-party governments but also within the EU institutions. Participants included representatives of a controversial separatist movement, the European Parliament rapporteur for relations in the conflict region, civil society, Member State representatives as well as representatives from EU foreign and diplomatic service. The QCEA facilitator opened the session by providing ground rules of confidentiality and inviting participants to a 'tour de table', where every participant introduces her/himself and her/his organisation, to ensure everyone was aware of who was in the room. The aim of the meeting was to provide a safe space to help build trust between EU officials and representatives of the occupied territory given the relationship had degraded following a controversial report published by the EU on the region. By bringing people together around a table in a peaceful atmosphere, QCEA showed its ability to use quiet diplomacy and build common ground. The discussion took place as an international organisation was leading a dialogue

amongst stakeholders in the region. Despite disagreements during the event, common ground was identified at the end of the meeting on support to the international organisation's process, which provided space for actors to hold follow-up meetings. QCEA wanted to create a space in Brussels for people who don't normally meet in this type of setting. Most of QCEA's work takes place over a series of events but this was a one-off event, so it makes for a different example.

(Olivia Caeymaex, paper prepared for
the Woodbrooke consultation, 2019)

QUNO had prepared a paper for the consultation that included details of work undertaken by David Atwood, a former director of QUNO Geneva. This example illustrated the impact of a long-term piece of conciliation work carried out during the period 1995–2011:

QUNO's involvement in the work to ban anti-personnel landmines was an unlikely turn of events. During my orientation to go to Geneva in late 1994, I was told that, of all the possible disarmament issues that I might explore, I should probably stay away from landmines as, even at that stage, there were 500 or so organisations around the world that had joined the International Campaign to Ban Landmines (ICBL). When I arrived in Geneva in early 1995, there had been no disarmament program at QUNO for nearly two years. One of the necessary components for working effectively in Geneva or New York or in other policy settings is to be credible, to have something to bring to the policy process. This is not automatic. Where to begin? A period of scoping was necessary. This included attending in Vienna the first ever Review Conference of the Convention on Conventional Weapons (CCW) in the autumn of 1995, where I met key members of the ICBL and, despite advice to the contrary, found myself drawn to this new, dynamic international movement. Several months later, while still looking to re-establish an involvement in disarmament affairs, QUNO joined the email network for the ICBL (a new communication tool in the mid-90s for social movements). The ICBL leadership, at that time, noted that there was a need to test the expressed interest of a number of governments in going beyond the likely outcome of the continuing CCW deliberations. The call from ICBL was for someone to pull these so-called 'good guy' governments together to check their credentials and intentions in relation to an outright ban on anti-personnel landmines. I immediately thought, "We can do that. This is exactly the kind of thing QUNO is here to do." And so, on a damp evening in April 1996, Quaker House [Geneva] hosted a totally off-the-record meeting of representatives of those governments that had indicated their wish for a stronger outcome than the CCW proceedings would produce. At that meeting the government of Canada put on the table the idea of hosting a meeting later in the year in Ottawa to see what might be done further.

And the rest is history.

The new Convention on the Prohibition of the Use, Stockpiling, Production and Transfer of Anti-Personnel Mines and on their Destruction was signed by 122 states in December 1997 and entered into force just over a year later in early 1999. The ICBL and its coordinator Jody Williams were jointly awarded the Nobel Peace Prize in 1997. The recognition of QUNO's part in the achievement of this historic treaty led to my being invited as a member of the ICBL delegation to the Nobel Peace Prize ceremony in Oslo.

What seems important is to note a number of key lessons from this experience: QUNO's reputation in multilateral fields in general, and the reputation of Quaker House for off-the-record meetings in particular, enabled QUNO to contribute to an important global process even though we brought no specific expertise at the time of our initial engagement. Taking sides can be a legitimate strategy for QUNO. In this case, QUNO took sides with victims of the indiscriminate use of anti-personnel mines and joined with like-minded organisations and governments to assist in the development of this new global norm. Supporting the UN does not necessarily mean supporting existing institutions where they are clearly inadequate. In this case, we worked to support the evolution of a new institutional mechanism aimed at overcoming the weaknesses of the existing one. Despite the number of organisations working on the landmines problem, QUNO found its niche. And when the processes became robust enough to stand on their own and needed no further substantial contribution from QUNO, we withdrew from active involvement and turned our attention to other issues. The evolution of effective new global norms takes a long time. But once the right combination of the key factors of effective research, credible and effective organising, government/civil society partnerships and engagement by actors across the spectrum from local to global are in place, results can sometimes come much sooner than expected.

('The serendipity of presence: QUNO and the banning of
anti-personnel landmines', paper prepared for
the Woodbrooke consultation, 2019)

The strands running through these examples of work demonstrate the ways in which staff were able to build trust and personal connections by listening. Conciliators can offer support and create safe off-the-record spaces for those involved in the negotiations, who can often feel isolated and either restricted by or not sure about their instructions from their home government.

At Woodbrooke, these sessions were followed by plenary discussions that considered the need for long-term frameworks and the relevance of this type of work in a changing world. The discussions also considered the strengths and opportunities for the conciliation process beyond international institutions, and the importance of being knowledgeable about the needs and aspirations of the people with whom conciliators are working. It was recognised that conciliation is not the only tool; as described by Andrew Tomlinson, director of QUNO New York, "conciliation is one part of the whole orchestra of peacemaking".

Another section of this orchestra is empowering communities to develop skills relating to a nonviolent approach to conflict.

Turning the Tide East Africa

Benard Agona, the national coordinator of Turning the Tide East Africa, spoke about his organisation, which is involved with social action training. Turning the Tide is a programme developed by QPSW in the 1990s. It aims to "work alongside people to explore hopes, ideas and collective power to undertake imaginative, nonviolent action for positive social change" (Turning the Tide, 2019). When Kenyan Quakers approached QPSW for assistance with dealing with post-election violence, it was suggested that Turning the Tide might provide this assistance. Britain Yearly Meeting trainers adapted material developed in Britain to their needs and trained an initial group of Kenyan trainers. The programme has been developed within Kenya, and since 2010 it has grown to encompass seven staff and 45 volunteers. The programme was extended to Rwanda and Burundi in 2015, and Rwanda now has four staff and 19 volunteers while Burundi has three staff and 20 volunteers. Trainers undergo three weeks of intensive training spread over a long period of time, combining theory with practice. Once they have completed the course, they undertake ongoing training to upgrade their knowledge and skills.

Agona outlined the ways in which, as a grassroots organisation, Turning the Tide East Africa continues to train workers, select issues to work on and develop the programme most appropriately. It concentrates on helping communities to focus on a small aspect of a major issue, which helps to make the issue manageable and easier to cope with. This leads to a focus on real and practical issues with clear goals, strategies and timelines, enabling "individuals to be the change they want to see in the world".

Turning the Tide East Africa is guided by seven principles of nonviolence, which are built on Quaker beliefs and testimonies:

- Be willing to take action for justice without using violence.
- Respect and care for everyone involved in conflict, including your opponent.
- Refuse to harm, damage or degrade people, living things or the earth as a means of achieving your goals.
- Act in ways consistent with the ends we seek: peace and justice.
- Be ready to take suffering on yourself rather than inflicting it on others.
- Believe that everyone is capable of change and no one has a monopoly of the truth.
- Recognise the importance of training so that nonviolence thinking and behaviour become part of our everyday life.

Turning the Tide East Africa is guided by seven principles of nonviolence, which are built on Quaker beliefs and testimonies.

To illustrate Turning the Tide's methods, Agona gave a number of examples of ways in which local communities have addressed sources of conflict. These examples included one each from Burundi and Rwanda – two countries recovering from violent civil wars and where communities are fighting corruption and violence at a local level. The first story he provided was from Burundi:

> The issue was that corruption was widely spread (e.g. giving bribes for service), the abduction and torture of local people by the police. The campaign commenced with the Turning the Tide trainers holding meetings with members of the community and authorities, which led to the organisation of a large community gathering. As a result of the discussions the local head of social security was fired, as were two lawyers, and four politicians were dismissed. There was a decrease in corruption levels and an end of the torture in prisons. They were developing sustainable, grassroots initiatives; building collective community responsibility. This is less likely to be destroyed and becomes a way of life for those who have gone through the process.
>
> (Benard Agona, paper prepared for the Woodbrooke consultation, 2019)

The second example was from Rwanda:

> Rwanda was facing cultural violence against women and children. Men were selling the family property without informing (consulting) other family members. This had led to severe family conflicts; 93 families being displaced, and 200 children had dropped out of school. The campaign led to Turning the Tide training a group drawn from the communities and 60 meetings were held in different areas

and a large community gathering was arranged to talk about the issues. The result was that over 500 came to the gathering and Turning the Tide facilitators brought the issues to the surface and then helped the communities to take them forward. They helped to develop the inner strengths existing within them, which led to positive outcomes.

(Benard Agona, paper prepared for
the Woodbrooke consultation, 2019)

Agona concluded his talk with details of what Turning the Tide East Africa, as an organisation, had learnt from its experiences:

- Sustainable peace and justice can be achieved easily through a grassroots approach.
- Community ownership leads to more sustainable results.
- Conflict analysis by community members is key.
- Break down big problems into manageable issues to inspire action.
- To build strong and stable nonviolent movements, you need: exchange visits, experience sharing, sharing of success stories, working on similar issues, training and strategic planning.
- Small actions but BIG MOVEMENT.
- Nonviolent work calls for some spirituality: you need to have faith and believe that it is possible.
- Be flexible and willing to change the plan.
- Training is key for effective nonviolent campaigning. People need to be helped to start thinking and doing things differently.
- Incorporate other peacebuilding tools – nonviolent actions work best together with peacebuilding.
- Work with your opponents.

(Benard Agona, paper prepared for
the Woodbrooke consultation, 2019)

Following Agona's talk, the participants moved into small groups to share thoughts and reactions. They then returned to a plenary session to discuss the impact of Turning the Tide East Africa and whether the model could be spread out across the continent. There was also discussion about links between conciliation and Turning the Tide focusing on the connection between conciliation and campaigning, both of which contribute to societal transformation. Can campaigners be involved with conciliation? Does one form of intervention impede the work of the other? Agona said that there are close links between Turning the Tide and the peace committees in both Burundi and Rwanda, with collaborative efforts using approaches that are appropriate to each situation. The sessions concluded with discussion about the possibility of bringing the learning back to Britain at a time when its society is fracturing.

Ability of Quakers to respond to requests for help with conciliation

The ability of Quakers to respond to requests for help with conciliation was a major theme running through the conference. Participants highlighted the importance of international conciliation work. One person with whom Quaker international conciliators are currently working said that the support was invaluable: "We feel that the Quakers are behind us – supporting us. They have given us inner strength." Stuart Morton, another participant, spoke of a conversation he had had with a local leader while he was involved with a conciliation process. Stuart asked why they had wanted to work with Quakers. The response was, "Lots of people come here once but don't come back, but Quakers didn't follow that pattern."

While there was recognition of the strength of Quakers' capacity to respond in past and present programmes, concern was expressed about their ability to respond to future requests. Any such work would require not only a pool of people to do it but also the organisational resources to support it.

It was recognised that with the reduction of Quakers' international work, many of the links have diminished. However, there remains a network of connections that might in the future bring requests for assistance. It was also acknowledged that in the past, Quakers undertook this work at a time when other organisations were not involved. Now, there are numerous other organisations – both faith-based and secular – undertaking international conciliation, many of them with close links to Quakers. The situation was compared with Quakers' heavy involvement in humanitarian relief efforts. In this area, other organisations, often founded by Quakers, have grown and professionalised the work, releasing Quakers to move on to other types of activity.

However, Quakers continue to make and maintain connections through existing work. It is valued, and Quakers should be ready to respond when asked. One of the purposes of the conference was to share the skills and experience of past and present conciliators with "younger people who have already demonstrated interest" (Conference paper). All those representing the next generation at the conference had a wide range of skills, including campaigning, peace work and conciliation experience in secular organisations.

They presented their thoughts in a paper called 'Young people's thoughts on conciliation', which opened with the following statement:

Future conciliation work needs to change. A concern we hear is the urgent need for something in the UK. All of us in this room would potentially be up for being involved.

They outlined their vision for future conciliation work, which included:

- Bringing on new people to conciliation teams as mentees, rather than expecting full commitment from people who are still great but just don't have time – many of us thought this would be a great opportunity.
- For the discussion to be more fruitful we need to have a longer time frame to talk about everything. We feel rushed into learning so much and then having to make decisions, and we acknowledge that we need more time if we want to make decisions with integrity. So much will be lost if this event is the only moment to discuss the future of conciliation. Some of us are new to the work.
- When we think about whether we are able to respond to openings, we have to ask where are our gifts as a Society of Friends? Would we want to be able to say 'yes' if asked [to undertake new work]? … [We need] a process that is transparent, and that [gives us] the ability to say yes when asked.
- Having a pool of people for conciliation would mean opening up the process for nominations. Being more inclusive means letting people know about opportunities for being involved.

These young people had a desire to participate in future Quaker international conciliation and a willingness to join the pool of people ready to engage in training programmes. However, this desire and willingness were set within the recognition that at the present point in their own career paths, it would not be possible for them to commit the necessary time or respond to sudden or unexpected requests to travel. Nevertheless, there followed an exploration of the possibility of them being appointed to the relevant committees as non-travelling members. This would enable them to contribute and learn from others, possibly through a mentoring process so that, when the time was right, they would be able to participate in future international conciliation activity. Their contribution to this discussion was reflected in the final minute (see the appendix for the full text):

> We recognise the importance of Quaker processes and the need for them to be flexible and timely to respond to the needs and demands of the work in order to attract a diversity of Quakers going forward. There is a strong need to strengthen the pool of Quakers to work in international conciliation and offer opportunities for younger Friends including mentoring. We believe we have an initial pool among those present. A group of young Friends prepared a paper on their views on conciliation work. If Quakers were asked now to provide support for conciliation in a new international setting there is a sense that this should be tested and that we should be able to say yes. Quakers with conciliation experience working in non-Quaker settings asked for a facilitated network to support and offer opportunities to meet, share and learn.
>
> (Jenny Amery and Martin Macpherson, minute from the intergenerational exchange event for Quaker peacemakers looking at international conciliation work, Woodbrooke consultation, 2019)

The conference attendees were aware that a number of those present were, as Quakers, involved in international conciliation for secular organisations. Their need for support became apparent, and discussions considered how this might be given. It was felt that there was a need for a Quaker support network with links to QPSW. How this might function was uncertain. However, there was support for the idea of forming such a group, taking into account the different stages individuals are at in their careers, and the conference attendees hoped that it would happen.

This identification of the need to support Quakers working in secular conciliation organisations also highlighted the more general resource needs of Quaker international conciliation. Most of the work is undertaken by volunteer committee members, who give their time to keep abreast of developments in the areas in which they are working on a daily basis, but are also ready to travel to the region in question if the need arises. This work is based on past and ongoing links and relationships, which need to be maintained within the structure of Britain Yearly Meeting. With the reduction of Britain Yearly Meeting's commitment to international work, this has become more difficult. International work, including conciliation, has always been a part of Quakers' expression of their faith in action in the world. Not only do Quakers need to support the next generation to continue the work but they also need to educate and encourage the members of Britain Yearly Meeting at national and local level to support and continue a commitment to international work.

As the participants reflected on their learning over the days of the conference, there was a sense that there was much that had been discussed that could be applied to Britain. The participants recognised that in a fracturing society there is a need to address the underlying issues, and there might be a role for Quakers to contribute to this process. The skills and knowledge amassed over the years through international conciliation – such as working in 'small circles' at QUNO and QCEA and the Turning the Tide East Africa programme – have much to offer. They constitute a toolbox that Quakers might use within Britain at a time of increasing violence and intolerance.

The energy within the group of participants moved the conference forward at great speed. There were moments of joy and also of frustration. Everybody learnt much from each other, and it was quite clear that if Britain Yearly Meeting has the desire to continue this work, there is a pool of skilled and enthusiastic members of the next generation of Quakers to take it forward.

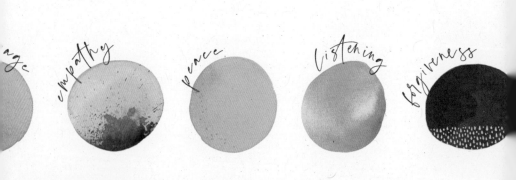

...age   empathy   peace   listening   forgiveness

Appendix

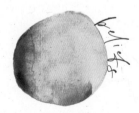

Minute from the intergenerational exchange event for Quaker peacemakers looking at international conciliation work, held at Woodbrooke, 15–18 September 2019

We have gathered as a diverse group with experience in government, intergovernmental organisations, QUNO and QCEA, Friends in education and community-based groups. We have been inspired by what we have heard from two colleagues from other countries working on conciliation and peacebuilding. We have been challenged and our thinking has evolved. This event arose in response to QPSW Central Committee minute 16/11 ('Quaker conciliation work'), which asked staff to develop a pool of Quaker conciliation practitioners. An intergenerational event was held at Woodbrooke 15–18 September 2019 for an exchange among Quaker peacemakers about international conciliation work, to capture the learning in a publication aimed primarily at British Quakers, and to collect ideas for future conciliation work.

For the purposes of the event we defined conciliation as "the process of bringing people together and creating enough trust between them for them to talk constructively together. It usually involves the help of facilitators to encourage the parties to move to that point and to engage in dialogue to resolve the conflict that has divided them." We explored what is distinctive about Quaker conciliation. As a group we are aware of the risks of overpraising Quaker conciliation and not recognising the values and qualities in other people's work. Some of the distinctive qualities of Quaker conciliation include its spiritual nature, our testimonies, living our values in all we do, a focus on listening to the needs of others, the long-term nature of our engagement and responding flexibly, and endeavouring to model an alternative world view to one that creates conflict and violence. We are aware of the risks in conciliation work, especially to those with whom we work. When considering opportunities for conciliation we need to ask ourselves whether we are the right people. We must be aware of Britain's colonial legacy and its implications for the present. In addition, we should consider the extent to which we can engage with others working in this space with different approaches.

After three days together there is a sense of excitement of learning from and building on the past – an evolution. In doing so we acknowledge our differences and discomforts. We aspire to grow and move forward together, younger and older Friends, sharing a common hope. We recognise the importance of Quaker processes and the need for them to be flexible and timely to respond to the needs and demands of the work in order to attract a diversity of Quakers going forward. There is a strong need to strengthen the pool of Quakers to work in international conciliation and offer opportunities for younger Friends including mentoring. We believe we have an initial pool among those present. A group of young Friends prepared a paper on their views on conciliation work. If Quakers were asked now to provide support for conciliation in a new international setting there is a sense that this should be tested and that we should be able to say yes. Quakers with conciliation experience working in non-Quaker settings asked for a facilitated network to support and offer opportunities to meet, share and learn.

We have also heard about the need for conciliation work in Britain and the importance of exploring opportunities in our communities. We were reminded of the role of embedded Friends in international settings and we recognise that we are embedded Friends able to witness in our societies. We sense a passion and determination to take this work forward, without expecting QPSW to assume all responsibility, and recognise that there are others who are willing to engage. Early on we were challenged to reimagine the future of Quaker conciliation work. We have a sense of leaving this space with hope, as a new people.

(Jenny Amery and Martin Macpherson, co-clerks of the QPSW Conciliation Group)

Participants at the Woodbrooke consultation

Adam Drury
Agona Benard
Aküm Longchari
Andrew Clark
Andrew Lane
Anne Bennett
Cassidy McKenna
Charlotte Cooper
Clem McCartney
Dan Silvey
David Mowat
David Newton
Diana Francis
Ellie McCarthy
Ellis Brooks
Faith Biddle
Florence Foster
Ivan Hutnik
Izzy Cartwright
Jan Arriens
Jenny Amery

Joe Jukes
John Lampen
Jonathan Woolley
Jordan Street
Judith Baker
Judith Large
Justine Taylor
Louice Wildfeldt-Lomas
Lyndsay Burtonshaw
Lynn Finnegan
Marigold Bentley
Martin Macpherson
Nick Lewer
Oliver Robertson
Olivia Caeymaex
Philip Wood
Rachel Clogg
Sam Walton
Simon Fisher
Stuart Morton
Tobias Wellner

Opposite: participants' photo, by Kate McNally

A poem by a participant at the Woodbrooke consultation

Conciliators reconciled?

Woodbrooke, where geese
Don't give way to joggers
And a torrent of traffic rises
With the sun and ebbs at dusk,
When Eton messes in bowls and papers
Are more, or less, digested,
A gaggle of reconciling Quakers come
To ponder on their craft;
Their destiny? Their epitaph?

Bold youth eye the floor, taken by the veterans
Who proclaim values of an earlier age?
Hero tales, our Indiana Jones the brave
Who asked Gestapo to let the people go.
The nights of foot-on-neck extend and we again
Would venture where angels fear to tread –
A Maison Quaker by a tyrant's bed
In Damascus? We discuss
And re-imagine Quaker roads for peace
Reaffirming qualities which, not unique,
Help fit our purpose, reach our peak:

"We journey in common hope as learners
Listeners questioners family
Immersed in unfamiliar lands
Not rushing, long-distance, truth-questing
Then building trust! Whether we
With diplomats dine or gunmen pray
Train up trainers, at meetings hold sway,
The front line we accompany
Compassed by a light within
Not as ministry staff behind bullet-proof glass;
Ours, a ministry of presence
Presenting love's transforming power
Contagiously, this very hour,
Persistently, drip by drip."

Up speak the young peacemakers:

"Never mind the mystery
Give us practical theory!
What's the end point? We need to know
If we should stay or we should go.
Your missions creep and strain
Without a robust logframe.
Where's the challenge-function,
Is it group-think at each junction?
We want to join you but is peace work lodged
For the volunteering privileged?

And wherever you may roam
Conciliation begins at home.
As for your non-communication
Over-caution, naïve belief that you are neutral,
We are conflict actors too!
Though they are many we are few."

And so we heard and shared four days
Sometimes in hope, sometimes afeared
Whilst tired, yet yearning for renaissance
An exhilarated welcome
Not to the darkness of the tomb
But emergence from
The womb.

David Mowat, 18 September 2019

GLOSSARY

A glossary of terms used at the Woodbrooke consultation and in Quaker conciliation work

Others define these terms differently, but for our purposes the following have been found to be most useful.

Conciliation: The process of bringing people together and creating enough trust between them for them to talk constructively together. It usually involves the help of facilitators to encourage the parties to move to that point and to engage in dialogue to resolve the conflict that has divided them.

Confidence-building: Activities that aim to increase transparency, trust and confidence among those who had been involved in a violent conflict.

Diaspora: A scattered population whose origin lies in a separate geographic place.

Ecumenical accompaniment: The model used by the Ecumenical Accompaniment Programme in Palestine and Israel (EAPPI) to seek an end to the occupation of Palestine. EAPPI is a World Council of Churches initiative that is run in the UK and Ireland by Britain Yearly Meeting on behalf of ecumenical partners. Since 2002 it has trained volunteers to provide a protective presence, support Palestinian and Israeli peace activists, and monitor human rights abuses. Find out more at www.eappi.org.

Facilitation: Enabling and supporting a group to achieve their objectives in a way that involves and respects all contributions, builds ownership by participants, and empowers them to carry out their decisions. It helps differentiate between process and content.

'Hearts and minds prepared': A Quaker expression for being in a suitable state for meeting for worship. It appears in Britain Yearly Meeting's *Advices & queries* number 9 (see https://qfp.quaker.org.uk/chapter/1).

'Hold in the light': To make certain that the work is guided by prayerful consideration and is open to unexpected shifts in perception or direction. To hold someone in the light is an old Quaker phrase. To many it represents God's love; the person is the object of deep, loving and active concern. See http://philipgulley.com/wp-content/uploads/2013/07/Quaker-Sayings-9-SECURE.pdf.

Institutions: QUNO and QCEA work with institutions such as the United Nations and its bodies, the European Union, the Council of Europe, the North Atlantic Treaty Organisation (NATO), and the Organisation for Security and Cooperation in Europe (OSCE).

Leading: In the Quaker sense, a leading is an inner prompting believed to be from the Holy Spirit.

Mediation: Third-party facilitation of negotiations between conflicting parties to resolve conflict and promote reconciliation. This may take the forms of shuttle mediation, meeting the parties separately, or face-to-face mediation. It is different from 'good offices', which are intermediary efforts to encourage parties to move towards concerted negotiations.

Nonviolence: A way of actively confronting injustice – not doing nothing, not responding violently, not running away, but struggling creatively to transform the situation. It is about doing conflict better; bringing about change without doing harm.

Peace education: This promotes the knowledge and skills to think critically about the root causes of violence and war. It teaches the values and attitudes needed to equip children and young people with the skills to help build peace and justice, at intrapersonal, interpersonal, intergroup, national and international levels. Find out more at www.quaker.org.uk/peace-education.

Peacebuilding: This includes a range of activities, working with those involved in the conflict at many levels, addressing their concerns and grievances in order to build a sustainable peace.

Peacekeeping: This is designed to ensure that an agreement is monitored. Peacekeepers monitor local activity and are ready to use force if necessary.

Peacemaking: This is the process of finding a way to end violent conflict that leads to an agreement that is acceptable to all parties. It may include political, diplomatic or military intervention and takes a form that is appropriate to the situation.

Peer mediation: Mediation for young people by young people, usually in schools. A peer mediator has been trained in the process of helping people in dispute to find their own solution. Find out more at www.peermediationnetwork.org.uk.

Principled impartiality: A deliberate decision not to take sides in a conflict, but to support human rights and international humanitarian law. This entails finding sympathetic ways to draw on the need for all sides to examine the extent to which they are respecting these principles.

Quaker Council for European Affairs (QCEA): A Brussels-based organisation founded in 1979 that works to bring a vision based on the Quaker commitment to peace, justice and equality. QCEA's peace and human rights programmes engage with the European Union and other European institutions. Find out more at www. qcea.org.

Quaker testimony: Quaker testimonies arise from an inner conviction, maintained and renewed over generations by personal experience and action. They are a way rather than a form of words, although there are written versions. Find out more at www.quaker. org.uk/our-values.

Quaker United Nations Office (QUNO): Based in New York and Geneva since 1947 and 1948 respectively, QUNO provides a Quaker presence at the United Nations. It works to represent Quaker concerns for global peace, human rights, sustainability, and economic justice. Find out more at www.quno.org.

'Quiet diplomacy': Quakers use this phrase to mean an inclusive approach to international negotiation, where the goal is to find common ground and a path forward. This extends beyond the common good to what is right and just and true. All discussion is strictly off-the-record and conducted in privacy.

Reconciliation: The restoration of relationships that have been broken; a process requiring the resolution of conflict and addressing the wrongs of the past so that all concerned can move forward together.

Shuttle mediation: This is when mediators work with all those involved without them all being together in the same place.

Witness: Quakers use this word to mean the process of living out our faith, as in 'to bear witness to something' – to speak out for it or to show it in action or in a way of living. Quaker Peace & Social Witness (QPSW), a department of Britain Yearly Meeting, is one example of its use in the Quaker context.

BIBLIOGRAPHY

American Friends Service Committee (1970). *Search for peace in the Middle East*. Philadelphia: American Friends Service Committee.

Bailey, Sydney (1989). 'Quaker peacemaking' in *The Friend*, 147(19), 585–586.

Bennett, Anne (2015). *To trust a spark: Living links with community peacebuilders in former Yugoslavia – A Quaker initiative*. London: Post Yugoslav Peace Link.

Britain Yearly Meeting (2013). *Quaker faith & practice*. Fifth edition. London: Yearly Meeting of the Religious Society of Friends (Quakers) in Britain.

Fisher, Simon, Dekha Ibrahim Abdi, Jawed Ludin, Richard Smith, Steve Williams, and Sue Williams (2000). *Working with conflict: Skills and strategies for action*. London: Zed Books.

Lampen, John (2011). *Answering the violence: Encounters with perpetrators*. Pendle Hill Pamphlet 412. Wallingford, PA: Pendle Hill Publications.

Mendl, Wolf (1974). *Prophets and reconcilers: Reflections on the Quaker peace testimony*. Swarthmore Lecture. London: Friends Home Service Committee.

Phillips, Brian (2006). 'Quaker global witness in the twenty-first century' in Brian Phillips with John Lampen, eds., *Endeavours to mend: Perspectives on British Quaker work in the world today* (pp. 9–24). London: Quaker Books.

Turning the Tide (2019). 'About us', Turning the Tide, www.turningtide.org.uk/about-us, accessed 13 December 2019.

Williams, Sue and Steve Williams (1994). *Being in the middle by being at the edge: Quaker experience of non-official political mediation.* York: William Sessions.

Yarrow, C. H. Mike (1978). *Quaker experiences in international conciliation.* London: Yale University Press.